The Elements of Autobiography and Life Narratives

The Elements of Composition Series
Series Editor: William A. Covino, Florida Atlantic University

David Blakesley
The Elements of Dramatism

Edward P. J. Corbett and Rosa A. Eberly
The Elements of Reasoning, Second Edition

William A. Covino
The Elements of Persuasion

Catherine L. Hobbs
The Elements of Autobiography and Life Narratives

Robert Funk, Elizabeth McMahan, and Susan Day
The Elements of Grammar for Writers

Elizabeth McMahan, Robert Funk, and Susan Day
The Elements of Writing about Literature and Film

Thomas E. Pearsall
The Elements of Technical Writing, Second Edition

Mariolina Rizzi Salvatori and Patricia Donahue
The Elements (and Pleasures) of Difficulty

Heidi Schultz
The Elements of Electronic Communication

William Strunk, Jr., and E. B. White
The Elements of Style, Fourth Edition

Bradford T. Stull
The Elements of Figurative Language

The Elements of Autobiography and Life Narratives

Catherine L. Hobbs

University of Oklahoma

New York • San Francisco • Boston
London • Toronto • Sydney • Tokyo • Singapore • Madrid
Mexico City • Munich • Paris • Cape Town • Hong Kong • Montreal

Senior Vice President and Publisher: Joseph Opiela
Vice President and Publisher: Eben W. Ludlow
Marketing Manager: Wendy Albert
Production Manager: Ellen MacElree
Project Coordination, Text Design, and Electronic Page Makeup:
    Stratford Publishing Services, Inc.
Cover Designer/Manager: John Callahan
Manufacturing Manager: Mary Fischer
Printer and Binder: R.R. Donnelley & Sons Company
Cover Printer: Coral Graphic Services

Library of Congress Cataloging-in-Publication Data

Hobbs, Catherine.
    The elements of autobiography and life narratives / Catherine L. Hobbs.
        p. cm
    Includes bibliographical references.
    ISBN 0-321-10562-1
        1. Autobiography—Authorship   2. Biography as a literary form.
I. Title.

    CT25.H63 2005
    808'.06692—dc22   2004016750

Please visit us at http://www.ablongman.com

ISBN 0-321-10562-1

    3 4 5 6 7 8 9 10—DOH—07 06 05

To Mark A. Mills

Contents

4 Autobiography, Media, and Technology: Old and New   81

Preface

What could be simpler to understand than the act of people writing about what they know best, their own lives? But this apparently simple act is anything but simple, for the writer becomes, in the act of writing, both the observing subject and the object of investigation, remembrance, and contemplation.
                                    —Smith and Watson, 2001

The *Elements of Autobiography and Life Narratives* is intended to help undergraduate students and teachers of writing understand and write life narratives—or, more accurately, to help them *improve* their writing of autobiography and memoir, as most of us already have had some experience with personal or life writing. Self-life-writing, as it was once called, is presented here as a means of self-expression as well as a way to grow, by developing insight into our lives. Unlike some approaches, however, this text works not to develop "true selves" or "authentic voices" but rather to make manifest and explore the diverse voices and subjectivities we all have in response to the complexities and fragmentation of life in these postmodern times.

Unlike some theoretical approaches, this book—while not afraid to acknowledge the difficulties of maintaining a seamless self—takes up recent notions about how people perform their "selves" in apparently unified, if not always completely harmonious fashion in their everyday lives. This concept highlights the importance of making probable judgments about complex personal and social issues—issues that may push our complex selves first one way and then the other, and then, it is hoped, draw us together as we take action to solve problems in our local and global worlds.

In order to achieve these aims, this book actively explores the elements of autobiography. Those elements consist in large measure of the arts of invention and arrangement—as we say in rhetorical terms— as well as what is effectively a new expansion of the classical rhetorical canon of memory. These arts are placed in social and cultural contexts with the Autobiographical "I"—as produced in relationship to other humans and their institutions, including literary traditions. The book hopes to lead the writer to examine how these social contexts, races, relationships, genres, genders, scripts, and styles have contributed to shaping his or her "self." It also prompts the writer to consider how various media—from colored pens and journals to photography and digital hypertext—are being and can be used in life writing as well as how the media act to shape writers and their narratives.

In the past few decades, literary theorists have questioned or dismissed traditional notions of a unified, private self. This critique has coincided with (perhaps even produced, in its wake or in reaction) a flourishing of life narratives—autobiography, memoir, family history, and newer digital genres that are unique in publishing history. A paradoxical convergence of sophisticated theory with the seemingly mundane genre of life narrative, not long ago scorned by literary critics, has made the act of writing in autobiographical genres more theoretically challenging and yet rewarding. Many questions about the elements of autobiography are raised in writing or teaching life writing:

- Who is this self that writes—as opposed to the self that is written about, investigated, or contemplated?

- How has the writer framed the Autobiographical "I"—specifically, through what social and institutional settings, in addition to the personal roles elicited there, including but not limited to the church, the university, the family, the peer group, the workplace?

- How would shifting the frame change the script?

- What stories is the writer allowed or encouraged to tell? How do pre-existing cultural scripts enter in (the Hulk, John Wayne, Cinderella, Star Wars, Beauty and the Beast, to name just a few examples)?

- Can the writer rewrite these narratives, resist them, or tactically renegotiate them, or is he or she doomed to repeat them with only slight variations?

- Conversely, what if a writer chooses to repeat and relive a traditional plot? Will the instructor and other readers accept that?

- With all these potential restraints, is it really possible for life writing to serve as a liberatory practice?

- Can autobiography help writers understand, frame and reframe their life experiences, reflect more productively, and grow and mature?

- Can autobiographical writing help students imagine more possibilities for their futures?

- Can it help us as teachers and students of writing to think more critically about our pasts as well as our present lives and experiences?

- Might reading and writing autobiographically help us be more tolerant of differences in others as well as in ourselves?

Such questions lie behind the practices of life writing presented in this book, and they are addressed at key points in the chapters. Yet they do not touch on a central motivation of many writers of autobiography and memoir: the sheer pleasure of forming the text as object, the "flow" state of creativity, the fascination with our mind's networks of memory, the satisfactions of working on, even descending through, painful and difficult material and creating something—a written product most often meant to be shared with others. I hope these pleasures and accomplishments will be visible in the book, as much as the intellectual issues presented here, as primary elements of autobiography.

A Word to Students about Life Writing

I read slowly through The Second Sex *by Simone de Beauvoir. Out of that thick dense book one line remains for me, and that line was worth the entire reading. "In order to create you have to be deeply rooted in the society." She said this to show why white males, rather than women or minorities, were in the forefront of art. She gave me the key to creative energy in that line, "To be deeply rooted in the society." To write I had to have my fist deep in my life—in my pain, my joy, my culture, my generation. In other words, I had to be alive. I couldn't be shut away in the kitchen or in the bedroom. I couldn't*

*protect myself from money, or cars, or politics. Writing is
the willingness to see. I had to be willing to look.*
—Goldberg, 1993

This book is designed to teach you more about the genre of autobiography and life narrative while helping you actually write life narratives. It presents suggestions and exercises to get you started, along with examples from other students to inspire you to write your own life stories. The chapters move from close-up shots of early remembrances to long shots of phases of your growing up and on to projections of your future life.

The book assumes that you not only are capable but are responsible enough to decide how "personal," how private you want your writing to be when it is to be shared with others. Being willing to reveal an inner self without censoring is important to growth in life writing. You may find, however, that revealing some experiences to yourself in a journal or to close friends or family is enough. Group experience with autobiographical writing should not feel like "forced confession." This book's orientation toward civic issues offers you a wide spectrum of ways to engage the personal.

Michel Foucault (1990, 58) writes that "since the Middle Ages at least, Western societies have established the confession as one of the main rituals we rely on for the production of truth." He observes further:

> We have since become a singularly confessing society. The confession has spread its effects far and wide. It plays a part in justice, medicine, education, family relationships, and love relationships, in the most ordinary affairs of everyday life, and in the most solemn rites; one confesses one's crimes, one's sins, one's thoughts and desires, one's illnesses and troubles; one goes about telling with the greatest precision, whatever is most difficult to tell. One confesses in public and in private, to one's parents, one's educators, one's doctor, to those one loves; one admits to oneself, in pleasure and in pain, things it would be impossible to tell anyone else, the things people write books about. One confesses—or is forced to confess. (59)

What is more, he says, confessions are "a ritual that unfolds within a power relationship, for one does not confess without the presence (or the virtual presence) of a partner who is not simply the interlocutor but the authority who requires the confession, prescribes and appreciates it, and intervenes" (63).

As a professor at a state university, I cannot help thinking about the power relations among people because of the institutional structure in which we find ourselves. I think it is worth reflecting on in autobiographical writing classes. Will we be able to subvert these forces somehow and create a space for mutuality and interchange? From my previous experience with students, I believe the answer is yes. I also know as I read papers and finally give grades that many contradictions exist when students undertake autobiographical writing. Yet I keep the faith and maintain hope. These issues would make an interesting discussion with your classmates.

Now, to the writing! If you start with Chapter 1 of this book and seriously engage the exercises and assignments across the chapters, as a whole or in part, you will end up with a life writing portfolio that will repay your efforts. My students often have been surprised when they put their pieces together and found that the whole was truly more than the sum of the parts. Compiling your work allows you to see the patterns in the whole. Even if you never publish your writing, I hope you will share your work with those closest to you. My former students have treasured their life writing portfolios and have grown in the process of producing them, and I hope you will, too.

Initial Advice to Life Writers

Seriously consider keeping a daily journal, by hand or on the computer, writing whatever you like whenever it strikes you or at appointed times, mornings and/or evenings. (I like to keep small spiral-bound notebooks that easily fit in my bag, but experiment until you find what suits you.) What should you write? It depends on your purposes, but some writers note events of the day, their responses to them, and reflections on whatever crosses their minds while writing. Other writers sometimes do "exercises" in their journals, such as describing what they see around them as they write or doing 10-minute "free writes" on particular memories or topics. Whether you want to present your material in a website or use it for personal growth, therapeutic, or social purposes, or as "data" for the basis of fiction writing, journaling and the other activities in this book are designed to help you get launched into self-writing with a variety of inventional prompts and projects.

Acknowledgments

I am grateful to all my friends, colleagues, and students who have encouraged or inspired me to share my work on autobiographies, or my autobiographical writing itself. Specifically, I thank William A. Covino, who initiated this book, and Eben Ludlow and his assistants at Longman, who provided suggestions and had faith in the project throughout. Thanks also to my colleagues who reviewed the manuscript and made suggestions, especially to Susan Laird, Susan Kates, and to Laura Gibbs, my "technical specialist," who helped with Chapter 4. Thanks to my OU School of Education colleague, neighbor, and scholar of autobiography Irene Karpiak for sharing her work. Also to the reviewers for Longman who made many valuable suggestions: Theresa L. Kulbaga, The Ohio State University; and Bradford T. Stull, River College.

Thanks are also due to my classes in advanced composition and autobiographical writing at the University of Oklahoma, particularly to those who shared their work: Tina Black Berry, Kevin Fischer, Autumn Glave, Janson Jones, Kelsey Martin-Farewell, Monica Guadelupe Gomez, Bobbi Story Miller, Bonner Slayton, and Tara Stine. I am also thankful for the support of David Mair, Department of English chair, and to Julie Gozan, who inspired me to begin.

I am especially grateful to my parents and family, especially my older brother Stephen, who collaborated on my earliest memories and provided pictures and family history, as well as to my close friend Mark A. Mills and his mother Martha, cofounder of the Oklahoma Writing Project in 1978, who knows a thing or two about autobiographical writing and has been wonderfully supportive.

Catherine L. Hobbs

1

Autobiography and Its Elements

*Our working definition of autobiographical or life narra-
tive, rather than specifying its rules as a genre or form,
understands it as a historically situated practice of self-
representation.*
                                        —*Smith and Watson, 2001*

Elements of Autobiography and Life Narratives takes a social and historical approach to life writing, such as described in the foregoing
quotation. This means that we will pay attention to the personal, of
course, but we will also look to the social and institutional contexts that
frame our stories in time. These social and institutional contexts might
be family; religious organizations; schools; friends; the media; economic, consumer, or work environments; politics; or the many other
contexts you experience. All can be considered as either local—lying
quite close to home—or as forces acting globally. Such an approach
seems warranted because it mirrors reality in all its elaborate interweb-
bing. Because of life's complexity, most of us experience our own lives
only partially—we cannot write about our birth with any more authority than our biographer could, and it goes without saying that we do not
know how the story ends. We do know, that our culture and most of its

institutions will go on after we depart. Now, however, we *can* get in touch with how we experience the world from the inside and translate this into the form of written life narrative, gaining insights into ourselves and our worlds as we write.

Defining Autobiography and Life Narrative

Like Smith and Watson (2001), quoted earlier, French scholar of autobiography Philippe Lejeune (1982) describes autobiographical writing as more than a genre that can be captured by a set of characteristics or rules. He argues that autobiography results from an unwritten "pact" between writers and their readers since the narrative is a true story about the author's life. This "autobiographical pact" is sealed by the author's signature, a signal that the author, narrator, and protagonist of the narrative are the same person.

Lejeune defines autobiography proper as a "retrospective prose narrative written by a real person concerning his own existence, where the focus is his individual life, in particular, the story of his personality" (4).

His definition makes four points:

- The form of language must be narrative and prose.
- The subject treated must be the individual life story of a personality.
- The author and narrator must be identical.
- The narrator and main character must be identical, and the narrator must take a retrospective point of view toward the past. (4)

In his closely reasoned definition, Lejeune separates memoir from autobiography proper because memoirs often present events and characters *witnessed* by the author rather than centering on reflections concerning his or her personal development. Autobiographical poetry does not count for Lejeune, nor do journals and diaries; in fact, autobiographical essays may not count if they do not meet the strict condition of being a retrospective of the author's life. For Lejeune, the question "Who am I?" in an autobiographical text is "answered by a narrative that tells 'how I became who I am'" (124).

Finally, however, Lejeune takes the perspective of a reader trying to make sense of the mass of published texts in the world. This is why he defines the genre in the "autobiographical pact" between the reader and the text. Autobiography thus becomes a mode of reading as much as a literary genre. He focuses on "the implicit or explicit contract proposed by the *author* to the *reader*, a contract which determines the mode of reading of the text and engenders the effects, which, attributed to the text, seem to us to define it as autobiography" (29).

In other words, the autobiography's author makes an agreement with himself or herself as constructed in the text to "incite the real reader" to join the "game" of reading and constructing the autobiography (126).

With this "reader-response" position toward autobiography, Lejeune recognizes that it is the reader who will bring the text to life and make it function. The autobiographical pact with readers holds writers to certain standards of truth in the telling. Clearly, the author, narrator, and protagonist—the central character of your writing—will be identical under the autobiographical pact. Within this pact, in this autobiographical space, the writing is true to life.

This textbook uses less stringent differentiations between autobiography and memoir but generally agrees with Lejeune's reader-based definition and arguments. It uses the term *life writing* to refer to a broad range of stories about people's lives, from memoir and autobiography to oral accounts told to others and biography. Other terms that may be used throughout the book are briefly defined here.

Autobiography/Life Writing Definitions

Autobiographical writing—writing that focuses on the experiences and standpoint of the writer, often using "I" to convey to readers what it is like to think, see, and feel life inside his or her skin.

Autobiography (two definitions)—"Retrospective prose narrative written by a real person concerning his own existence, where the focus is his individual life, in particular, the story of his personality" (Lejeune, 1982, 4). "A particular practice of life narrative that emerged in the Enlightenment and has become canonical in the West. . . . Privileged as the definitive achievement of a mode of life narrative, 'autobiography' celebrates the autonomous individual and the universalizing life story" (Smith and Watson, 2001, 3).

Autoethnography—related to the chief method of anthropological investigation, ethnography—literally, culture-writing. When we write autoethnography, we situate ourselves within the structure and power relationships of our cultures, seeing ourselves primarily as community or group members. The term is also frequently invoked in relation to postcolonial studies and travel writing.

Chronicle—a loose list of events in chronological order; formerly, lists of kings and battles that made early histories and served as the basis for later narrative histories.

Conversion narrative—a story centered on (usually spiritual) transformation; the pattern "once I was *X*, now I am *Y*." Smith and Watson (2001) list several, including John Bunyan's *Pilgrim's Progress*, which became a paradigm for such narratives in American literature (205).

Diary/Journal—life writing that is penned daily or sporadically in a variety of modes, always chronological. Some say the journal is less personal than the diary. The drama and interest of this writing occurs by accretion and by the fact that neither the author nor the reader knows what will happen next. Personal blogs (web logs) have this same dramatic structure when they are produced as daily journals on a web page.

Life narrative—a general term referring to any writing that tells the story of a life over time, including biographies, novels, and histories. *Narrative* refers to the form of a story told about events happening over time.

Life writing—a general term for writing about lives in various disciplines and modes.

Manifesto—a personal or collaborative position paper publicly announcing the author's or group's stance on controversies involving ethics, moral values, or cultural or political matters.

Memoir—the term traditionally assigned to autobiographical narratives that do not focus on the writer's personality as much as on what the author witnessed in his or her historical time; often descriptions of events or people. Lejeune (1982) and other authors separate the memoir from the autobiography proper, while others, such as Annie Dillard (Dillard and Conley, 1995), do not.

Trauma narrative—Leigh Gilmore (2001) notes that the Greek root of *trauma* is "wound." Trauma writing explores wounds that are often beyond language, and the effort to name and articulate such experience serves as an act of therapy for the writer.

Travel writing—a form of narrative that is deeply ethnographic, often combining outward description with personal reflection upon contact with a foreign setting and culture.

Language, Culture, Material Reality, Identity

> *Language, for the individual consciousness, is on the borderline between oneself and the other. The word in language is half someone else's.*
>
> —*Mikhail Bakhtin, 1981*

Our identities emerge from within a community, for communities produce identities: We discover who we are and what we have to say through life and dialog with others. Whom we identify with helps construct our identities, and this is brought about in large part through language. The language we use to speak and write is not at first our own. It comes from our cultures, beginning, for most of us, with our mothers. That is why the first language we speak has long been called the "mother tongue." (In the West, this was traditionally contrasted with the language of schooling, or Latin.)

In large measure, we did not invent our terms, our metaphors, or our commonplaces. As the early twentieth-century literary theorist Mikhail Bakhtin (1981) explains, before we appropriate language, "it exists in other people's mouths, in other people's contexts, serving other people's intentions: it is from there that one must take the word and make it one's own" (293–94). In this same way, we must also wrestle with conventional forms and genres we receive through our cultures, for each generation must learn and, in the process, remake these structures for themselves. Anthropologists and literary theorists have shown how the everyday stories and forms we take up for our unique and individual lives come from our cultures, often delivered to us first as common fairy tales and children's stories.

The technologies we use to produce our life narratives also play a role in how our stories are told. We may write our stories differently for a blog or a personal web page than for our paper journals, even if our journals are not private but are meant to be shared. *How* we are saying *what* to *whom* affects what we can and will say. In addition to the elements of language, forms, and media, other key elements of our life stories include sociological "facts" such as race, age, gender, geography, and class. I will have more to say about these elements in later chapters.

Mind and Inner Speech

Because so many factors interact with the stories we will tell, we may wonder, "Who are we, if not our stories?" Perhaps, as it has been proposed, we are our memories. But how reliable are our mental faculties? Somehow we sense that our memory is not always reliable. *Then who am I anyway?* This is the sort of complicated question that pops up as we do what was once scorned as a fairly low-level intellectual act—writing personal and family narratives. Today we know that autobiography is as artful as literature and as nuanced and difficult to write and criticize. Much of the complexity arises with the issues of identity or subjectivity.

Who we are involves our body-mind, and we can see its mark or trace in our writing. When we write, we use language that not only reveals who we are generally, but also helps construct and solidify who we are at the very moment we are writing. The texts we produce can be revised. Does this mean we are revising our *selves*? These interesting philosophical questions cannot be answered definitively, but they can be observed in practice. Writing makes subjective experience materially available for contemplation.

The tradition of journal writing uses writing to observe—and sometimes change—the mind. Journal writing most often involves freewriting of the sort you may have already done in school. The idea is to take a topic, avoid self-censoring, and just begin to write, usually for a brief period of time; 10 minutes is a good warm-up time.

Those who work in the journaling tradition—for example, the Taos autobiographical writer and painter Natalie Goldberg—often begin a writing session with silent meditation. This technique of stilling and observing the mind is ancient. Although Goldberg follows that tradition as a Buddhist nun, Christianity also has a centuries-old tradition of prayer and meditation. Early Christian meditation often attempted to convert the invisible to the visible by calling on the seeker to place himself or herself on the scene, to "see the spot"—such as the stable where Christ was born—or to imagine settings for abstract ideas such as sin or redemption (as described by writing specialists Rohman and Wlecke, 1964). These processes allowed the mind to focus, settle, and produce a personal experience to better grasp the abstract notion.

A later theorist of writing, calling consciousness "that great ongoing inner panorama," explained in the 1980s: "Writing and meditating are naturally allied activities. . . . inner speech and meditation concern forms of thought, the composing of mind that constitutes the real art and worth of writing" (James Moffett, 1982, 231). This process is easier to experience than to describe. If you are willing to try it, you may gain an understanding of your mind's potential.

▶ *Silent Meditation*

Sit quietly, cross-legged on a cushion on the floor or in a comfortable chair. Tune into the sounds around you, your heartbeat, the state of your body. Acknowledge what is going on around you, but accept it and let it be. When you become comfortable, begin to focus on your breath as it travels into and out of your body. Focus your attention on wherever the breath manifests itself—in your nose or in the rising and falling of your diaphragm and chest. Do not attempt to control the breath, but try only to observe it. You might note in a low, interior voice the processes of "in" and "out." When thoughts come to you, note them in the same detached manner. You can simply label them nonjudgmentally, with terms like *thinking* or *planning*. Then let them cross the threshold of your consciousness like clouds floating by, returning your focus to the breath. Similarly, note emotions, but let them pass like the weather. Sit for 10 minutes at first, although you may want to lengthen the time to 20 minutes as a preparation for daily writing. Journal writing is a good activity to engage in immediately after a silent meditation. ◀

▶ *Write Now! Journaling*

After your first meditation, free-write in your journal for 10 minutes, noting what you experienced and what you observed about your body and mind. Was your mind active, jumping from thought to thought like a monkey swinging from limb to limb? This is so common that meditators call it "monkey mind." Rohman and Wlecke (1964) connect it with autistic tendencies of the mind. Also consider whether your breathing was smooth, raspy, deep, or shallow.

Have you ever considered that along with the journals, computers, pens, ink, and other paraphernalia of writing, your body-mind is what you have to work with in writing—the most important piece of "technology" you have? Writing classes should pay much more attention to getting in touch with this key element of life writing. ◀

Memory: A Key but Complex Element

> *"Memory is a field full of psychological ruins," wrote French philosopher Gaston Bachelard. For some, that may be true, but memory is also a field of healing that has the capacity to restore the world, not only for the one person who recollects, but for cultures as well. When a person says "I remember," all things are possible.*
> —Linda Hogan, 2001

It is not for nothing that brief focused pieces of autobiography are called "memoirs." Unless we are lucky enough to have extensive journals, notes, and diaries, (and perhaps even if we do), we rely heavily on our memories in personal writing. Yet those who study memory are finding that it is not like videotape—it is uncertain, easily influenced, and malleable. It is interesting that scholars are finding that memory does not "set" until about the age we learn language, which seems to give it a firmer scaffolding or structure. We do have nonverbal memories, of course, but even those may be firmly linked to our language system.

This means that if something happens to you at or before age two, you may not remember it. But if you grow up with family members repeating the story at dinner repeatedly, you may feel that you have a clear memory of the event. You may have distinct pictures in your mind, recall sensory events, and believe you have a clear consciousness of being there. Some people believe memory always works this way. So, are we our memories? Two centuries ago, the Scottish commonsense school of philosophers believed that the "clear and distinct" contents of their memories were the basis for rational thought. Today, we are not so sure.

Cognitive Models of Memory

New theories of memory question the reliability and unchanging nature of the "commonsense" beliefs about memory. According to the latest theories, based on neurological and psychological research, the brain is not a photo album in which memories are stored discretely like unchanging photos, as Jonathan Franzen (2001) has written in a *New Yorker* memoir about his father's Alzheimer's disease. Memory is a "temporary constellation" of activity, shuttling around a neural network that binds sensory images and semantic data into the "momentary sensation of a remembered whole." The brain relies on preexisting categories, like "red" and "heart," and images of significant figures and experiences, like "mother."

In the latest model, memory is a "set of hardwired neuronal connections among the pertinent regions of the brain, and a predisposition for the entire constellation to light up—chemically, electrically—when any one part of the circuit is stimulated" (Franzen, 2001). This is similar to what John Locke and later eighteenth-century speculative thinkers noticed and called "associationism." Franzen notes that one of the great adaptive virtues of our brains—surprisingly, why our brains are better than computers—is our ability to forget. We retain general categorical memories but few specific, episodic memories. When we revisit memories, we strengthen the neural network, making it a more permanent part of the brain.

Another feature of the mind is its predisposition to construct wholes out of fragmentary parts. We constantly fill in blanks—in our visual fields and in our conceptual perception of reality. That is why memory is not really experience. We are explorers mapping territory from memory, but as is frequently noted, "the map is not the territory." One problem is that part of the map might be filled in to represent what has not really been explored by us at all. It is amazing that the mind's ability to fill these gaps and perceive the whole works as well as it does to get us through our daily lives. It seems that what is probable or makes sense as part of a pattern often has enough truth to it that it can function in practice like the real thing when we can't get our hands on the actual Real Thing. Stories are patterns of narratives, and we are a tissue of stories. This can have us puzzling, however, over the relation of narrative truth to scientific truth—for example, the map that is created from satellite photography. Yet even the complex scientific truth about our lived experience would still be meaningless and useless to us without being distilled into narrative truth. So we must throw ourselves upon the resources of memory and its close relative, imagination.

We know that there are limits of language and limits of perception, along with the limits of memory. In many fortuitous ways, we are not our memories. Franzen (2001) seems to believe there is a strength of "will" that exists beneath the level of memory, forming the core of personal identity. This core of will in his father helped shape the course of his Alzheimer's disease, allowing him to retain some control of himself and also to relinquish that control when he chose to let go and face the end. Experiencing this sense he calls "will" enabled Franzen to argue against the brain's being a mechanical, computational device. Writers should be the last people to believe in the brain and its memory as simple machines.

Cultural Memory and Life Writing

Another memoir about memory itself is Linda Hogan's *The Woman Who Watches Over the World* (2001). A Chickasaw whose family hails from near Ardmore in Oklahoma, Hogan tells stories from her life focusing on memory and culture, bringing together personal and cultural memory of both pain and healing.

Personally, language for Hogan becomes a way to transcend and transform the pain of loss and the pain of disease and injury into hope. Her life has so many challenges: a sexual relationship at age 12 with a man three times her age at the German army base where her family lived, fibromyalgia, and the experience of adopting two seriously abused Indian girls, one of whom is so seriously damaged that Hogan likens her at one point to a feral child—the daughter who can never recover.

Finally, a throw from a horse breaks bones up and down Hogan's body and leaves her with a closed head injury and permanent memory damage. Yet her exploration of her memory problems is interwoven with the pain of loss of native values and way of life. The pain of her actual loss of memories and serious physical damage seems to symbolize the cultural pain—the loss and forgetting of languages, rituals, stories, religions, communities, and other missing aspects of Native American culture.

But how does one trust a memoir written by one who confesses to having a damaged sensorium? How can cultural memories, many from oral cultures that have been lost or suppressed, be returned, revivified, and represented? This is something writers of many groups struggle with. Perhaps that is why many autobiographers are criticized for having misrepresented a culture when they bear the burden of speaking as a representative member.

Plato criticized writing in his dialogue *Phaedrus* as being only a "crutch of memory." He feared it would destroy memory itself, not realizing that memory is culturally different in each historical era. Plato lamented the decline of the oral tradition and the atrophy of memory that writing produces. Yet it is our will to record permanently, to set down our stories in more or less permanent words, that Franzen sees as making us larger than our biologies.

Hogan relies on writing to fix her memory. She reads the words she has written in the hospital, where she was unconscious for a week then in a semicomatose state for many weeks more. She has no memory of writing those words, yet they stare her in the face and tell stories of who was at her side, the kindnesses they performed for her, the visions she saw while in her altered state. She reads the mythical stories of the native peoples, of the Greeks, and interweaves their memories with her own. She asks her parents questions and records the stories they tell her, stories she needs to get down to remember, to heal. Remembering and healing go hand in hand here as in many important life narratives. This is true for people as individuals and as members of a variety of groups, especially those at the margins whose cultures' memories are often not valued or encouraged by dominant groups.

▶ *Write Now!* "*I Remember . . .* "

> *When a person says "I remember," all things are possible.*
> *There are ways in, journeys to the center of a life, through time, through air, matter, dream, and thought. The ways in are not always mapped or charted, but sometimes being lost, if there is such a thing, is the sweetest place to be. And always, in this search, a person might find that she is already there, at the center of a world. It may be a broken world, but it is glorious nevertheless.*
>
> *—Linda Hogan, 2001*

How do we begin our journey into the center of our lives? Anne Lamott, in *Bird by Bird* (1995), talks of looking at life through a one-inch window. The beauty of this perspective for writing is that rather than making a heroic attempt to write sweeping movie epics, we take life "bird by bird," like Lamott's brother, who was overwhelmed at first by a school report on birds until he succeeded by the method suggested in her title.

What does this concept mean for your writing? Start with a one-inch window on memory, for example, and list what you can see. You can list anything, as long as it is something that strikes you in a memorable way—visually, verbally, emotionally. It could be your grandmother's teeth, your first memory of Christmas, what was in that closet your parents kept you out of, the first time you lost a tooth or held your baby sister, your old room—literally anything. After you make a fairly long list, write a paragraph each about three or four of the items on your list, adding as many sensory details as possible—minute things you could see, hear, smell, taste, feel, and experience about the item. Or write for 10 minutes on one of the following:

- My grandfather's (or grandmother's) chair
- My sixth-grade class
- My favorite (or first) car
- A room in my childhood home
- A favorite book or character in a book
- A pet from the past

Get out your journal and start with 10-minute writing sessions, then expand them to 20 minutes. What you write will sometimes be mundane and even worse, but there will be times that what you remember and write will surprise and amaze you.◀

Here is a short journal entry that represents the start of an essay I wrote on coffee rituals in my family.

Catherine Hobbs

"Coffee"

I grew up in a coffee family, an extended coffee family. All my grandparents, great-grandparents, aunts, uncles, and, naturally, my parents, drank coffee every morning and whenever else the coffee bug bit. Coffee was always made and offered if anyone dropped by to have a piece of pie or a cinnamon roll, and I never in my young life saw anyone turn down a cup of full-blooded, naturally caffeinated coffee.

One of the early markers of change in my life was when my dad, in his mid-thirties and perhaps gaining weight, left off taking sugar in his coffee and went to drinking it black like his father, who drank gallons of black coffee to accompany his Camels.

My coffee family liked their java perked, for many years on a gas stove. Coffee came in yellow and blue square packages or red coffee cans in two varieties, Cains and Folgers. There was a progression of percolators, from beat-up dull aluminum with the glass bulb serving as a window into the pulsating brew, to a laboratory-looking glass chamber, and finally to a gleaming, modern stainless steel electric pot, Farberware.

Grandad preferred his coffee made on the stove, and it had to be served to him at a boil in the cup. The cup itself must be thin china, so he could feel the heat. He "quaffed" it in so quickly that it never touched his mouth until it hit his uvula, by which point it had cooled. My own father today takes his coffee from an electric drip pot but has his own particularities about cups—the cup must have a handle big enough to get his fingers through and must be served three quarters full, neither more nor less. It is preferred that it be set down on the table and not handed to him.

I cannot recall for sure how the makers and servers of this coffee liked their brew. I believe my mother and grandmothers did not have time to be particular, but perhaps because they had chosen all the cups, it was all the same to them. Sometimes mother would take cream, but she usually drank hers like dad's. At my paternal grandparents, a visit meant a crowd of relatives sitting (and standing) around an old aluminum and formica kitchen table, drinking coffee and eating donuts fresh from the boiling oil, cinnamon rolls, pie, or cobbler. Needless to say, all my siblings took up drinking coffee sooner or later.

Today, I like my coffee strong, with half-and-half until it is just the color of cappuccino. I sometimes stray from the path, drinking hazelnut beans ground fresh, expressed with steam in an Italian pot, or dripped Starbucks. I always come back to Folgers, as the old commercial jingle promised (or maybe that was for Kent or some other brand of cigarettes). I am by now a lifetime addict, although recently I went through withdrawal for a week after embarking on a special weight-loss diet. But my two sisters came to town, nipping that miserable experiment in the bud. I couldn't eat pie, but I drank coffee, with cream, in my favorite cup at Mom and Dad's, a large white mug painted with a red Cheshire cat that disappears when hot coffee warms the china, leaving only a big blue smile.

Although an addict, I have a long way to go. I have never knowingly reached the 30-cup-per-day limit that Balzac was said to have drunk. But I have overindulged to the point of watching my eyeballs on the ceiling for hours at night in bed.

The other effect of overindulgence is a dreamy, staring look that so frightened the editor on my first newspaper job that he sent me to a doctor (who, somewhat oddly, gave me pills to slow down my digestion). Coffee sends me happily into the ozone while speeding up my language machine, a la Balzac. Perhaps that is why I write with a clear glass mug (wide enough for fingers, Dad was right) of caramel colored liquid beside me, cream added, followed by heat boosting in the microwave (Grandad was right). My "angel places" have been coffee shops where you can sit and visit with friends for hours, like the pre-Starbucks-era Coffee House in Normal, Illinois, or the defunct Lovelight in Norman, Oklahoma. Yes, coffee has taken me from Norman to Normal and back, and here I stand my grounds.

▶ *Write Now! Family Rituals, Memory Work*

Write your own memoir of a ritual in your family or group of close friends. At a loss? Interview parents and siblings. Raid the family archives. Go through a box of mementos or a collection or book of photos and write a list of memories from their visual cues. Art lovers can reflect on their memories of first encounters with favorite paintings or photographs. Watch an old movie and let it help you remember.

Culture and Memory: An Absent Presence

Here are some questions to discuss with your group or to free-write about in your journal:

- What memories have cultural value in your life? Why?

- What memories are not valued and privileged, and why?

- How does cultural memory shape personal memory and autobiographical narrative?
- How does national memory connect with your personal memory?

As an example, Caroline Chung Simpson's book about Japanese-Americans after World War II, called *An Absent Presence* (2001), takes its title from media critic Maria Sturken, who discussed the internment of Japanese-Americans during World War II as one "for which history provides images primarily through their absence."

Almost 120,000 people of Japanese ancestry, two-thirds of whom were Americans by birth, were incarcerated because of the suspicion by others, including the government, that they would be traitors after the bombing of Pearl Harbor by the Japanese in 1941. Our cultural memory of this shameful event and of Japanese-Americans' lives before the war is just now being revived in memoirs such as *Farewell to Manzanar*, by Jeanne Wakatsuki Houston and James D. Houston.

Japanese-American neighborhoods, entire towns, and family and individual heritage—especially on the West Coast—were scattered and lost after the arrest and detention of community leaders and families following the bombing of Pearl Harbor. Few family photos survived, as many families decided to hide and destroy scrapbooks and other mementos, fearing that government agents would misinterpret their existence as disloyal. Language schools closed, and religious life and symbols were suppressed. "The people and their culture were essentially forced into internal exile," as the Seattle Arts Commission's (2002) book presenting photographs of Seattle's Japanese-American landmarks put it. (Gail Lee Dubrow with Donna Graves)

I have found that the concept of an "absent presence" is a constant in cultural memoirs. For example, Azar Nafisi's memoir *Reading Lolita in Tehran* (2004), a recent and recommended best-seller about the author's years of college teaching in post-revolutionary Iran, makes use of the concept in writing about things that are no longer present in her life today. She looks at a photo of students and recalls the one who is not in the picture. "This is Tehran for me," she writes. "Its absences were more real than its presences."

- Is there an "absent presence" in your life? What historical gaps exist for you that might be attributable to cultural oppression or suppression?
- What is acutely present in your life because it is absent? ◀

Beginnings

It is often noted that there are two things no autobiographer can set down. One is certainly our own deaths. Because of how our memories work, however, we also can't write from personal experience about something we *were* present for, something wondrous and momentous—our births. Yet our origins frequently have a tremendous impact on who we are and what we might become. Even the raw statistic of our birth weight has been shown to correlate with our future development to some extent. Fatter babies are sometimes farther ahead developmentally and stay that way in life. Why this is so is not clear, although it is probably due to many factors, from general health and development to how parents treat a baby who is a weakling as opposed to one who is already a half-grown bouncing bundle of joy. Our sex is another example of initial factors that more or less determine our paths. How we begin our journey does matter, but not everyone knows how his or her life began. If your parents never discussed such matters, if you are adopted, or if your parents died without giving you information on your birth, you may have to speculate. Go ahead! No doubt you have already speculated anyway, so write it down now and begin the story.

▶ *Write Now! "I Was Born . . . "*

Interview your parents or whoever was around when you were born—aunts, uncles, godparents, doctors, or friends of your parents. Get as many details as you can. Get a copy of your birth certificate to check facts. What day of the week were you born? What time? Who delivered you? Don't forget to ask about sights, sounds, and emotions flooding the stage of your beginning. Basic facts might include where you were born, length at birth, weight, time of birth, duration of mother's labor, any stories leading up to labor, who was there, drugs or natural delivery, any crises, what happened next, and next. . . . When and where did you go to your first home? What did you wear home? Who first cared for you?

   Even if there is a silence around your birth, we still know that you were born! What if no one remembers your birth or there is no one to ask? This then becomes *your* birth story. Write what you know or suspect, how you came to be where you were raised, what you have done or might do to trace down the missing facts, and how you have adjusted to not knowing. ◀

▶ *Going Deeper: Five Chapters of Your Life*

If you were going to write a book-length autobiography—a full auto-biography, reflecting on your life as a whole—how would you plan and organize it? Write five chapter titles that you might use. Then begin on one of the chapters. Chapters can be organized chronologically or in other ways, thematically or metaphorically. For example, one of my students wrote an autobiographical work called *The Sycamore Tree*, describing her favorite place to hide as a child. Chapters such as "Roots" and "Branches" played on this image, as did her division of seasons. Try more than one set of titles. Do the chapter titles suggest a plot? Different approaches may suggest different emplotments. Do you find one plot more acceptable than another?

My colleague, Professor Irene Karpiak, teaches adults through auto-biographical writing. In one class at the University of Manitoba, early in her teaching, she asked students to write five chapters of their lives. "I encouraged them to avoid organizing their work as a simple chronology of events, and instead, to pay attention to any metaphors or patterns that emerged as they reflected upon each successive chapter" (Karpiak, 2001, 35). Here are some titles she got from her students that contain underlying metaphors:

- Learning To Be in Charge of My Own Plot
- Painting the Adult Canvas
- Friends: The Thread of Life
- And There's a Chance of . . . Blue Skies, Cloudbursts, Sunshine & Shadows, Shifting Winds, New Horizons (36)

One student wrote of the periods of her life as different colors:

Chapter One, Rose . . . a smudge on my rose-coloured glasses.

Chapter Two, Gray . . . If only the damned fog would lift.

Chapter Three, Black, The night that lasted 4½ years.

Chapter Four, Yellow, Let the sun shine in.

Chapter Five, Purple, Everything's coming up violets. (38)

Try writing some chapter titles that are descriptive of your life overall. Patterns may emerge in the process of working through this assignment that are not visible or available to you when you are working on a smaller canvas. ◀

Writing Autobiography: Autobiography as Rhetoric

From the beginning, we should remember that life narrative is rhetorical; that is, it attempts to persuade the reader, either overtly or subtly. (This is true even if a future "you" is the intended reader of a journal the present "you" writes today). Memoir relates and explains but also works to persuade the reader of the truth of a life, an experience, or an insight.

Rhetoric was the classical Greek and Roman science of speaking both eloquently and persuasively—in the law courts, the legislature, and the public forum. Classically, rhetoric is often illustrated by the use of a triangle, with the writer at one point, the readers at another point, and the text at the third point. (This triangle is often set in a circle, the historical and cultural horizon of the triangle.) The material of language is depicted in the center of the triangle. The Greek terms related to the corners of this triangle are *ethos, pathos*, and *logos. Ethos* is the credibility appeal, referring to the persuasiveness of a virtuous and credible speaker or writer; *pathos* represents the appeal to the emotions, attitudes, and values of an audience; and *logos* is the appeal to the reason or intellect of the audience in the text. (See Figure 1.1.)

The text itself (speech or autobiography) can be shown by another triangle, with the narrator at one corner, the protagonist at the second, and the "implied" readers at the remaining corner. This means that the narrator of the tale, the protagonist or hero, and the implied or imagined readers are created by the author and evoked through the writing.

The writer might actually intend the real reader to be himself or herself later in life. That person thus becomes the audience for the piece. Whatever audience is intended, consciously or not, traces of that audience are shaped in the writing. The difference in audience has been described as the real, addressed readers versus the audience invoked in the text. If you intend your family, friends, or unknown members of the public to read your book, these would be the real, addressed readers. In your mind, you are writing to an ideal reader—someone you intend to be sympathetic to

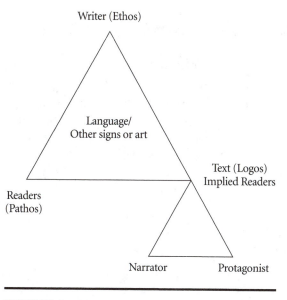

FIGURE 1.1

you, perhaps someone who understands adolescent angst and will accept your thoughts and actions as represented in your work. You will actually create a trace of this reader through your choice of materials and your voice—the invoked reader. Perhaps you fear a resisting reader and write argumentatively to overcome or overwhelm him and drag him into your net. This reader, too, will be invoked in your writing. When drafting or journaling, you may not be aware of the audiences for your writing, addressed or invoked. Writing group members can give you feedback on your implied reader. Perhaps they will refuse to take the role you give your textual reader if you talk down to them or whine. Perhaps your writing group members are not your ideal reader and cannot read your piece well at all. Those issues all have to be sorted out, but the process of doing so gives you a great deal of information about what you have produced and whether you are meeting your conscious intentions nonetheless.

Writing with Others

If you are in a class, your instructor will no doubt encourage you to work in small writing groups or in pairs, because the best writing and the most intense development in writers often comes out of a collaborative process. Writing teachers have long known this, and the latest research has verified that working with others in a friendly, supportive process of writing and revising can improve your writing (see Ede and Lunsford, 1992). What can you do if you are working outside a classroom setting? Take the initiative to form your own small writing group. You probably know at least one person who is interested in writing and in reading others' work. You can even work long distance via phone or email. But if you don't know anyone, most communities have writers' organizations that may break down into smaller writing groups. Ask at your local library. You might also be able to find people at a distance who can work with you via email and telephone.

Revising Autobiography and Memoir

Most good writing in the world takes place through a process of writing, reviewing, and then revising what is on the page. Often we don't know what we want to say when we begin or where the "center of gravity" of a piece will emerge. Revision is a big part of the creative process. But how do we read and evaluate writing we feel is almost or completely ready to share?

Here is a set of criteria you may use to read and respond to your fellow students' or group members' life narrative writing. In the beginning, you might not want to use the full set, but you could use one or two of the numbered sections at a time as a focus in reading others' life narratives. You can also use them to reflect anew on your own drafts.

▶ Revision Guide for Personal Essays

Reader's name:

Writer's name:

Title of Piece:

First Impression:

1. Focus, Purpose
   - What is the focus or center of gravity of this piece of life writing? (Remember, in narrative writing especially, the focus may not be explicitly stated as a thesis in an argument.)

- What promise does the writer make to the reader in the opening segment?
- What feeling do you get from the beginning? From the end?
- Does the piece sound as if the writer is exploring a matter of personal significance or marching through chronology?

2. Development
   - How does the writer support or develop this piece (e.g., examples and illustrations, descriptions, sensory details, anecdotes, statistics, quotes from others)? Is the development adequate for the readers and the situation? Is it appropriate to the focus?
   - Are there separate scenes, with setting and dialog?
   - Are there sections of summary and probing reflection after related events or narrative vignettes?

   Development for audience

   - Who is the intended audience? What role is the audience asked to play?
   - Is this role comfortable for you as a reader? Why or why not?
   - Does the paper as a whole deliver on the promise the writer makes in the beginning? What questions still bother you at the end? If you are satisfied, what makes you satisfied?

3. Organization
   - Is the organization of the paper chronological or thematic?
   - Are there clear scenes and summary passages, or is this an experimental order? When there are flashbacks, can the reader orient in time?
   - Is the organization effective for the focus, reader, and situation? Do the parts fit well, and are they clearly signaled?

4. Style (The language of personal experience is often concrete and imagistic, to evoke emotional response in the reader.)
   - How would you describe the language here?
   - Does the writer use effective sentence patterns? Do any sentences need breaking apart or combining?

   General editing for conciseness, when appropriate

   - Put all prepositional phrases in brackets. If many exist in one sentence, rewrite one or two to eliminate the prepositional phrase.

- Put an X through all *there, these, those,* and *this* sentence openers. Try rewriting one or two to see the difference.
- Underline all *to be* verbs. Rewrite one or two sentences, eliminating them if many are used and the essay seems to need more energy.

5. Conventions
    - Are there places where the writer has failed to use the conventions of standard written English—grammar, spelling, and punctuation?
    - Does this function as part of the essay's voice and tone, or is it just lack of mindfulness? ◄

2

The Autobiographical "I"

Suddenly everyone in the universe of literary critics and theorists seems to be talking about autobiography, a genre critics described until recently as a kind of flawed biography at worst, and at best a historiographical document capable of capturing the essence of a nation or the spirit of an age.

—*Sidonie Smith, 1987*

Along with a turn to the Osbournes and reality TV, Americans have added a related—perhaps healthier—taste for creative nonfiction in literature. "Suddenly it seems memoir has become *the* genre in the skittish period around the turn of the millennium," scholar of autobiography Leigh Gilmore (2001) writes. Her rough analysis of one global database showed that the number of English-language volumes classified as autobiography or memoir roughly tripled from the 1940s to the 1970s.

Writing magazines and journals are now filled with articles on autobiography and memoir; the most popular new genre in creative writing, called *creative nonfiction*, is autobiographical at its core. The *New Yorker* magazine often carries memoirs under the heading "Personal History," "Memory," or recently, "Family History." At the height of the memoir craze, the summer fiction double issue for June 17, 2002, was almost all memoir or family history, except for three short stories, two poems, and the usual spate of journalistic articles.

No doubt about it, autobiography and memoir have become favored genres in publishing over the past decade or two, along with such related books as biographies and autobiography-based fiction. The trend has become so intense that Margo Jefferson (March 14, 2004) wrote in the *New York Times Book Review*:

> "Don't bring us any more memoirs!" This is the new cry in the book industry, I'm told; and a foolish cry it is, unless what publishers no longer want are those unshaped tales written as though every detail mattered simply because it happened. (27)

Not only has the number of published memoirs increased, but the authors themselves have had a sea change. Whereas autobiographical genres were formerly written by people who were growing older and conducting retrospective analyses of their lives, today many young people are getting into the act.

Dave Eggers's first book, for example, was a lengthy best-seller called *A Heartbreaking Work of Staggering Genius*—about his experiences raising his brother after both his parents died within a month of each other when he was 21. He jokingly referred to his book as *Memoirs of a Catholic Boyhood*, in reference to Mary McCarthy's famous memoir, *Memories of a Catholic Girlhood*.

Other examples of younger memoirists' work that you may want to read include Mary Karr's *The Liar's Club: A Memoir*, Susanna Kaysen's *Girl Interrupted*, or Lucy Grealy's *Autobiography of a Face*. Some of these books are about traumatic childhoods, and the writers have produced them as part of a project to heal themselves or understand how their experiences have formed them. Sometimes this kind of writing can be healing, but at other times it simply feeds the writer's obsessive focus on the trauma. Yet autobiographical writing need not always be about traumatic or dramatic experiences. As the Jefferson quotation makes clear, the writing must be well shaped and about something that "matters." It is foremost a way to craft our heart's truth into art, to help us better understand and share our lives.

The Genre of Autobiography

As we have seen, autobiography or life narrative is writing that most often uses "I," although there are no hard and fast rules even about that.

Henry Adams wrote his famous autobiography, *The Education of Henry Adams*, in the third person—a distanced, objective form that perhaps allowed him to see himself as a historical person in the long Adams family lineage of presidents. We can trace the third-person autobiography back to the Italian philosopher Giambattista Vico's work in the early eighteenth century. Vico, rhetoric professor at the University of Naples, was asked to write an essay relating how he had been educated and describing his process of development as a philosopher. This kind of philosophical autobiography—now mostly written in the first person—has remained a key part of the genre, written especially by successful men, for three centuries.

Growing out of this tradition, autobiography proper attempts an overview of a life, a holistic retrospective, often seeking to judge and evaluate what has been learned and achieved. It has its conventional material: birth, family history, cultural and geographical context, first memories, education, and so forth. A good example of how old-fashioned the classical nineteenth-century genre sounds today is found in the German immigrant Oscar Ameringer's *If You Don't Weaken* (1940). However, I still love the big-voiced autobiography with its reminiscences of Oklahoma farm families in the hard-scrabble 1920s, which begins with a boom:

> Boom! Boom! Boom! One hundred booms. The cannons were thundering a salute impressive enough to announce the birth of a prince of the blood, but I was not a prince, even though I was about to be born. My mother heard the guns as she was busy making hay on one of her twelve acres in the bottom lands of the Danube valley. When the birth pangs came over her, she barely managed to load the hay and bring it, the wagon, the cows, and me safely home to Achstetten before I put in my appearance. . . . The occasion [for the salute] was the victory of the German forces in the battle of Spiechern Heights during the early days of the Franco-Prussian war.
> In those days, we lived, as I was born, under the sign of Mars. (3)

In contrast to the grand scale of traditional autobiography, what has traditionally been called "memoir" usually exists on a smaller scale, limited to a portion of life or some kind of "phase." As we have seen, in the strictest definitions, it has focused more on reporting what went on outside the writer than on seeking insights into the "autobiographical I." *Memories of a Catholic Girlhood* (1946), Mary McCarthy's autobiography or memoir, begins with an address to the reader in a different, more intimate voice than Ameringer's:

> These memories of mine have been collected slowly, over a period of years. Some readers, finding them in a magazine, have taken them for stories. The assumption that I have "made them up" is surprisingly prevalent, even among people who know me. "That Jewish grandmother of yours . . . !" Jewish friends have chided me, skeptically as though to say, "Come now, you don't expect us to believe that your grandmother was really Jewish." Indeed she was, and indeed I really had a wicked uncle who used to beat me. . . . (3)

McCarthy's separate chapters may more properly be called memoir, but put together, they compose an autobiography. Much of what is being written today can more properly be called memoir. The authors tell selected stories about a theme, phase, or series of related events, and segments of reflective essay writing link them and probe their meaning. Some make use of letters—including emails—and diaries, journals, poetry, and experimental forms. In the history of autobiography, memoir and these other forms are more often found in women's writing.

History of the Word Autobiography *in English*

Tracing the history of the word *autobiography* in English provides one window into the history of life writing. The term itself is constructed from the Greek by combining *graphe,* "to write," with *bios,* "life," in the sense of the course of life or way of living. *Auto* has the original meaning "of or by oneself," from *autos,* "self." So the word simply means the story of one's life, written by oneself.

Scholar of autobiography Robert Folkenflik (1993, 2) explains that a form of the English word was first used in print in 1786 by a woman poet, Ann Yearsley, who was derisively called Lactilla, the Milkmaid Poet. She used the term "Autobiographical Narrative" in a preface describing her troubled relationship with her patron, the writer Hannah More (coincidentally, the woman who invented Sunday schools).

In the West, before about the mid-seventeenth or beginning of the eighteenth centuries, most scholarly and literary writing was in Latin, the international academic language. (Of course, some famous authors such as Dante, Shakespeare, and Bacon had written in the vernacular before that, as had many women and less well educated men.) But when authors of the so-called Enlightenment era began writing more frequently in English and the other vernacular languages, it opened the door for women and others who were not trained in classical tongues. Problematically, however, the specialized terms were all in Greek or Latin, so-called inkhorn terms. Writers working in their mother tongues had to "invent" or rearrange words in those languages to provide English terms. So it took a while for the term *autobiography* to catch on.

The influential *Oxford English Dictionary* traces the word's history to Robert Southey in 1809, who wrote of Yearsley and others involved with life narratives. Thus, apparently, by the late eighteenth and early nineteenth centuries, a little band of writers had begun to use the term *autobiography*. Other forms such as *self-biography* contended for pride of place with *autobiography* but lost out to this term, once scorned as pedantic. The word entered English before other European languages had such a term, although each language has its own history with a term for autobiography. In Italian, for example, such a term was first recorded in a dictionary in 1828–29 but wasn't used commonly until much later. The German philosopher Schlegel used the term *Autobiographien* in 1798, but a term more like *self-biography* was usually used.

Schlegel had this interesting take on autobiographies and autobiographers:

> Pure autobiographies [*Autobiographien*] are written either by neurotics who are fascinated by their own ego [I], as in Rousseau's case; or by authors of a robust artistic or adventuresome self-love, such as Benvenuto Cellini; or by born historians who regard themselves only as material for historic art; or by women who also coquette with posterity; or by pedantic minds who want to bring even the most minute things in order before they die and cannot let themselves leave the world without commentaries. [They] can also be regarded as mere *plaidoyers* [legal pleadings] before the public. Another great group among the autobiographers [*Autobiographen*] is formed by the autopseusts [self-deceivers]. (quoted in Folkenflik, 1993, 3)

It is hard to quibble with this fiery description of autobiographers. Yet we must allow that there is another group—those of us who wish to examine the contents of our life and consciousness to come to understanding and insight. Surely ego is involved, and the quest is in some sense futile, for however much we write and gain enlightenment, we will still remain in most respects a mystery to ourselves and others.

About the literary critic Walter Benjamin's take on stories, Margo Jefferson (2004) writes:

> Every real story is useful, Benjamin wrote. The usefulness may lie in a moral, in practical advice or a series of probing questions. But in every case the storyteller is a man who has "counsel for his readers." And counsel, "woven into the fabric of real life, is wisdom."

▶ *Reflect Now!*

Think of autobiographical narratives—especially those of public figures—that you have read or seen as movies. How was the main character portrayed? What seemed to be the author's motivation for telling the narrative? Was there insight to be shared, an axe to grind? What might have been Mrs. Custer's motivation for writing her narrative of her life with George (*"Boots and Saddles": Or, Life in Dakota with General Custer*), for example. What other (perhaps higher?) motivations can you identify for writing autobiographically? ◀

History of the Genre of Autobiography in the West

Just as one might catch a disease before it has been named, one could write "autobiographically" before the word itself appeared. Describing a distinct tradition of women's autobiography, scholar Estelle Jelinek (1986) traces the earliest first-person narratives to the walls of Egyptian tombs in the Middle Kingdom (2000–1786 B.C.E.). Of course, these were not true autobiographies because they were not actually written by the people they were about. Later, however, an Egyptian daughter of a Pharaoh did dictate her life narrative. In the Hellenistic age of Greece, Sappho's love poems were autobiographical, and Alexander the Great began the practice of keeping diaries. Agrippina II, mother of Nero, wrote personal and familial memoirs (15–59 A.D.) Early autobiography often took the form of letters, such as Cicero's *Letters of Attica*, relating his experiences of being a consul.

Jelinek notes that in the tenth and eleventh centuries A.D., Japanese court women kept diaries and notebooks and also wrote personal poems and letters. Yet much of Eastern culture was opposed to individualism and might have seen autobiographical writing as immodest. Nonetheless, there were enough personal references in the court writings of Emperor K'ang-hsi (1661–1722) for Jonathan D. Spence to compile an entire first-person biography of his words, an act of personal auto/biography.

Thus, the term *autobiography* in English is distinctly modern; it was not used in the ancient world. This is not true, of course, of the term *biography*. A form of this word was first attributed to a Greek writer in the fifth century B.C.E. who wrote a biography of his tutor. *Biographia* was used in Latin but not in English until Dryden used it in 1683, discussing Plutarch's book of Greek and Roman lives. Another Englishman, Roger North, wrote biographies and an autobiography called "notes of me." He had a theory he termed "life-writing" and wrote of "idiography." He lived from 1653–1734 in what has been called the Age of Enlightenment—the era that spawned modern scientific and political thought.

Some would argue that autobiography arose in the Renaissance with the great Renaissance "lives" of Montaigne, Cellini, and Cardano, or would cite Augustine's earlier *Confessions*. Unlike Augustine's spiritual work, however, Rousseau's (secular) *Confessions*, written during the Enlightenment, reads like a novel and is named by nearly every scholar who has traced the history of autobiography. It is not surprising, then, that many scholars believe Rousseau when he says in his *Confessions* that he is the first modern autobiographer: "I have resolved on an enterprise which has no precedent, and which, once complete, will have no imitator. My purpose is to display to my kind a portrait in every way true to nature and the man I shall portray will be me myself."

Nevertheless, autobiography as a genre of writing is more often linked with the Romantic era following the Enlightenment, when individuality and originality became prized. The poet and literary theorist Coleridge used the term "self-biography," but it never took hold (so he switched to the hyphenated "auto-biography"). You may recall or be surprised to note that the 1847 novel *Jane Eyre* by Charlotte Brontë was subtitled "An Autobiography."

In the tradition of women's autobiographies in the West, Jelinek notes that several women wrote important early Christian autobiographical works, including Dame Julian of Norwich (1343–1416?), *Revelations of Divine Love*) and religious mystic Margery Burnham Kempe (1373–1438?). Kempe's life narrative was dictated to a neighbor in 1432. Theresa of Avila wrote her famous *Life* in the Renaissance, 1565–66. One of the first autobiographies by a woman to be explicitly called an auto-biography—*A True Relation of My Birth, Breeding, and Life*—was published in 1814 by Enlightenment figure Margaret Cavendish, Duchess of Newcastle (1622–99). As is true of several early women's autobiographies, she wrote her life narrative as part of a biography memorializing her husband. (Many of these early autobiographical works were not published until the nineteenth century.) Lady Anne Halkett (1622–99) was a master storyteller and so wrote a fine life story. One "notorious" eighteenth-century woman's memoir, "Memoirs of a Lady of Quality," was certainly read by Jane Austen, because it was published as a long chapter in Tobias Smollett's novel *Peregrine Pickle* (Lady Frances Anne Vane, 1713–88).

Autobiography flourished in the nineteenth century, when African Americans, many of whom had been banned from reading during slav-ery, wrote prolifically after the Civil War. Harriet Jacobs's *Incidents in the Life of a Slave Girl*, Frederick Douglass's great *Narrative of the Life*, and Booker T. Washington's *Up from Slavery* presaged the burst of life writ-ing and autobiographical fiction by writers of color in the twentieth century. Other nineteenth-century books included *The Autobiography of Mrs. Oliphant* (1899), the prolific British writer; American Margaret Fuller's *Woman in the Nineteenth Century* (1855), and Frances E. Willard's (1839–98) small but powerful work, *How I Learned to Ride the Bicycle: Reflections of an Influential 19th-Century Woman*.

Critical Studies of Autobiography

The genre of "modern" autobiography in the West is thus less than three centuries old. But consideration of autobiographies and other life nar-ratives as literature—by which I mean reading autobiographical work critically as literature—came quite recently. James Olney's introduction to his 1980 collection on autobiographies credits a 1956 essay by George Gusdorf as beginning the theory and criticism of autobiography. Olney's work itself began in the late 1960s and early 1970s. Historical and critical work on women's autobiographical writing often proceeded separately, with some arguing that women had a separate tradition.

A recent book, Smith and Watson's *Reading Autobiography* (2001), is one of the first textbooks to treat autobiography seriously as a literary genre to be taught in English classes. The book contains an appendix describing 52 genres of life narratives. Some examples of the genres— or "patterns for presenting self-knowledge" or "templates for autobiographical storytelling" (70)—are the bildungsroman (narrative of social development), the spiritual conversion narrative, the narrative of artistic growth, the slave narrative, and the journal or letter. Autofiction, "the French term for autobiographical fiction" (186), is also listed as a genre. With the teaching of autobiography as a literary object to judge and analyze as well as a legitimate genre of writing to produce, life writing has now truly come of age in the twenty-first century.

▶ *Reflect Now!*

At times, publishers have chosen to market certain works either as memoir or as fiction, and readers must make their own judgments. To cite a current example, many Republican commentators have called Hillary Clinton's memoir fiction, whereas Democrats rate the book highly as political memoir. Think of an example from your reading of a book that provoked controversy over issues of genre. ◀

Autobiography and Truth

> There is a place where the human enters dream and myth, and becomes a part of it, or maybe it is the other way around, when the story grows from the body and spirit of humankind. In any case, we are a story, each of us, a bundle of stories, some as false as phantom islands but believed in nevertheless. Some might be true.
> —Linda Hogan, 2001, 205

The aim of autobiography—to tell the true story of one's life— has become a complex project in this world, partly because of the ambiguities in the very origins of the genre. Fiction and autobiography have traded places since the novel began in the eighteenth century, when, as we have just seen, the modern constellation of genres called autobiography began as well. Was this a coincidence? (Perhaps you will want to speculate in discussion or writing on this historical intersecting of literary events.)

Nonfiction such as history or travel literature sold better than fiction in the eighteenth century, so novelists—including Defoe (*Journal of the Plague Year*), Melville (*Moby Dick*), and Poe (*The Narrative of A. Gordon Pym*)—sold some of their work as memoir (Dillard and Conley, 1995). In recent times, it has been more common to see auto-biography passed off as fiction. Louise Bogan published part of her memoir, *Journey Around My Room*, in the *New Yorker* as fiction. One chapter of Edward Dahlberg's memoir, *Because I Was Flesh*, appeared in *Best Short Stories of 1962*. (Dillard and Conley, 1995, xi) The line between fiction and autobiography or memoir has wavered, but the question of truth has remained the touchstone for autobiography. But what kind of truth *is* this autobiographical truth?

Conceptions of truth appropriate to autobiography have been dis-cussed in terms of three aspects: Does the autobiography correspond to historical fact? Does the text as object contain internal coherence and consistency? And is there a metaphorical truth to the autobiography, a truth of one sort linking faithfully to another quite different form of reality? Or perhaps autobiography is more like a painting, a self-portrait, linked similarly to early modern portraiture? In its overlap with the novel, does it merge with novelistic truth? Does its style reveal important aspects of the life truth? There are postmodern theorists, however—philosophers like Roland Barthes and Jacques Derrida—who proclaim the "death of the author" and believe that the interest is in the text itself. They therefore find that a focus on the particulars of the writer is beside the point.

At times, truth has been seen as a communal representation of real-ity rather than the truth of an individual's life. In the 1990s, Nobel Peace Prize winner Rigoberta Menchu wrote an autobiography, *I, Rigoberta Menchu: An Indian Woman in Guatemala*. The *New York Times* reported that the book contained events that Menchu had never actually experi-enced. Menchu countered that the events did occur, but she admitted that they were not always her personal experiences. She said she also wove in the experiences of others she knew, writing as a representative being to raise international awareness of the plight of her people in Guatemala. This composite experience, she argued, helped to make the book more true. This revelation caused a crisis among those who relied on her accounts to argue against U.S. policy in Latin America. The rupture of the "autobiographical pact" indeed can have consequences. Legitimate questions still remain about the truth of autobiography. Should life narratives be literally true, like journalism? Or should they be metaphorically true, providing oblique glimpses into deeper truths? Even if an autobiographical account is literally true, authors who bear the burden of speaking for an ethnic group can come in for criticism if others do not see their account as representative. Maxine Hong Kingston's *Woman Warrior* came in for criticism by some who claimed that she did not accurately depict Chinese culture. Her autobiography was in a novel, and some other authors also choose to call their autobiographical work fiction. Publishers have been known to reassign the term *memoir*, simply because it is likely to sell. "Autofiction" then seems like a term we need in English as well as in French.

A recent Broadway play by Nora Ephron centered on the conflict between Lillian Hellman and Mary McCarthy over autobiographical truth. As a novelist, McCarthy was always careful to test and separate in her memoir what she thought she actually remembered from what she might be fictionalizing. She was horrified at Hellman's beatific portrayal of the apparent rogue Dashiell Hammett in Hellman's memoirs. McCarthy once said of Hellman, "Everything she writes is a lie, including 'of' and 'the'." Hellman's memoirs, *Pentimento*, were found to be untrue when it was learned that she had never met the woman she wrote about who later became the subject of the film *Julia*. Hellman's reputation might have suffered more if she had not died soon after this untruth was revealed.

Truth is a central question that readers must confront in reading every autobiographical work. If you would like to read some classic and popular memoirs, not all of which are at every moment literally true, here are some suggestions: Benjamin Franklin's *Autobiography*; the *Narrative of the Life of Frederick Douglass*; Mark Twain's *Life on the Mississippi*; Booker T. Washington's *Up from Slavery*; Harriet Jacobs's *Incidents in the Life of a Slave Girl*; Jane Addams's *Twenty Years at Hull House*; Jack Kerouac's *On the Road*; Zora Neal Hurston's *Dust Tracks on a Road*; Margaret Mead's *Blackberry Winter*; *The Autobiography of Malcolm X*, with Alex Haley; Richard Rodriguez's *Hunger of Memory*; Mike Rose's *Lives on the Boundary*; Jeanne Wakatsuke Houston's *Farewell to Manzanar*; Frank Conroy's *Stop-time*; Harry Crews's

A Childhood; Kate Millett's *Flying*; Maya Angelou's *I Know Why the Caged Bird Sings*; Gloria Anzaldua's *Borderlands/LaFrontera: The New Mestiza*; Henry Louis Gates Jr.'s *Colored People*; Elinor Pruitt Stewart's *Letters of a Woman Homesteader*; Maxine Hong Kingston's *The Woman Warrior: Memoirs of a Girlhood Among Ghosts*; and Ghandi's *Life*.

If you are more inclined toward the classical genre of Western philosophical autobiographies, try some of these: *Autobiography of Giambattista Vico*; Hume's *Life of Himself*; John Stuart Mill's *Autobiography*; H. Spencer's *An Autobiography*; Nietzsche's *Ecce Homo*; Kierkegaard's *Journals*; Sartre's *Les Mots*; Russell's *My Philosophical Development*; and others that are part of the Library of Living Philosopher's Series, such as John Dewey's autobiography.

Other important women's autobiographies are Shirley Chisholm's *The Good Fight*; Ida Minerva Tarbell's *All in a Day's Work*; Emma Goldman's *Living My Life*; Margaret Sanger's *An Autobiography*; Gertrude Stein's *Autobiography of Alice B. Toklas*; Ida B. Wells-Barnett's *Crusade for Justice*; and Golda Meir's *My Life*.

Memory and Memoir, Fiction and Truth

In the December 24 and 31, 2001, *New Yorker*, Amy Tan had a short piece titled "My Mother" under the classification "Memory." When I read it, I thought, "I've seen this before!" I turned to the ending of Tan's novel *The Bonesetter's Daughter* and found that the kernel scene was almost word-for-word the same. In the *New Yorker* memoir, the author's mother is severely disabled by Alzheimer's disease but surprisingly rings her up on the telephone:

> "Amy," she said, and she began to speak quickly in Chinese. "Something is wrong with my mind. I think I'm going crazy."
>
> I caught my breath. Usually she could barely speak more than two words at a time. "Don't worry," I started to say.
>
> "It's true," she went on. "I feel like I can't remember many things. I can't remember what I did yesterday. I can't remember what happened a long time ago, what I did to you . . . " She spoke as a person might if she were drowning and had bobbed to the surface with the force of the will to live, only to see how far she had already drifted, how impossibly far she was from the shore.

She spoke frantically: "I know I did something to hurt you."

"You didn't," I said. "Really, don't worry."

"I did terrible things. But now I can't remember what. And I just want to tell you . . . I hope you can forget just as I've forgotten."

I tried to laugh, so that she wouldn't notice the cracks in my voice. "Really, don't worry."

"O.K., I just wanted you to know."

After we hung up, I cried, both happy and sad. I was again a sixteen-year-old, but the storm in my chest was gone.

My mother died six months later. But she had bequeathed to me her most healing words, those which are as open and eternal as a clear blue sky. Together, we knew in our hearts what we should remember, what we can forget.

In the epilogue to Tan's book *The Bonesetter's Daughter* (2001, 403) the author tells a parallel if not exact repetition of this memoir. In that passage, the narrator and her dead mother seem to merge to become the "author" of the story.

They write about what happened, why it happened, how they can make other things happen. They write stories of things that are but should not have been. They write about what could have been, what still might be. They write of a past that can be changed. After all, Bao Bomu says, what is the past but what we choose to remember?

Would *The Bonesetter's Daughter* be a better book if it were less auto-biographical? Should Tan's heart's truth about mothers and daughters that she learned through living—and through writing—be more distanced from her own personal story, as writers were once taught? Would it be more artful? I doubt it. Although it is interesting to link the memoir and the fiction, does it really matter if the novel speaks the truth if it is barely reworked memoir? In the genre marked autobiography, however, we know that the autobiographical pact with readers should not be broken without reason. There can be consequences: Breaking that pact revokes the motivation for writers to write self-life stories and especially for readers to read them. These are matters for discussion with your writing teachers and groups. My advice to you would be to label your writing "fiction" or "autofiction" if you will not dedicate yourself to seek and write true to the facts of your life when writing autobiography and memoir.

Perhaps the power of individual memory, at the juncture of our ancestors, cultural memory, and personal experience, may be linked to some mysterious quality or biological gift both Franzen and Tan call "will." Whatever this power of the self may be in these authors' narratives, it enabled Tan's incompetent mother to make a phone call, and Franzen's father to choose to let go of life and die. Perhaps it is the act of exploring this indefinable Will that makes it possible for life narrative to be an art of liberation for both writers and readers. Nonetheless, the "autobiographical I" in our writing, at our core, remains a mystery.

Language, and Writing from Names

> *"The name of the song is called 'Haddocks' Eyes.'"*
>
> *"Oh, that's the name of the song, is it?" Alice said, trying to feel interested.*
>
> *"No, you don't understand," the Knight said, looking a little vexed. "That's what the name is called. The name really is 'The Aged Aged Man.'"*
>
> *"Then I ought to have said, 'That's what the song is called'?" Alice corrected herself.*
>
> *"No, you oughtn't: that's quite another thing! The song is called 'Ways and Means': but that's only what it's called, you know!"*
>
> *"Well, what is the song, then?" said Alice, who was by this time completely bewildered.*
>
> *"I was coming to that," the Knight said. "The song really is 'A-sitting On a Gate': and the tune's my own invention."*
>
> —*Lewis Carroll, 1872*

Socrates said "Know Thyself." That might mean looking introspectively at yourself, but it could also mean looking at the link or hinge between your inner self and yourself as other people know you—by what you are called, your name! In *Text Book: An Introduction to Literary Language* (Scholes et al., 1995, 241), students are asked to think about proper names, beginning with the famous line in Juliet's soliloquy, "What's in a name? That which we call a rose/By any other name would smell as sweet." Of course, in *Romeo and Juliet*, being Romeo and a Montague means everything, for the plot hinges on a family feud.

If we are not our memories, are we perhaps our names? Our names may not dictate our destinies as much as the names of a Montague, an Adams, or a Rockefeller, but because people form impressions of us based on our names, our names, too, can influence our lives and identities. In "Hidden Name and Complex Fate," Ralph Ellison—Ralph *W.* Ellison—speculates on these matters for African Americans, particularly himself, Ralph Waldo Ellison. He noted that the familiar name caused him "no end of trouble" when he was growing up in Oklahoma just before World War I, leading many to tease him or call him Emerson instead of Ellison.

Slaves were often renamed with their owners' names, so some African Americans have adopted African or other names. Moreover, Latinos and Latinas keep their mothers' last names as part of their permanent names. Women also have problems with names, because historically, many women have changed their surnames when they marry. Such naming or unnaming practices make it difficult for many people to trace their genealogies and understand their heritage. For several decades now, traditional ways of naming have been transformed: Some women keep their surnames their entire lives and some families and individuals rename themselves at will. (I know one white, middle-class, female-headed family that took the surname "America" during the Bicentennial year.)

▶ *Reflect Now!*

We also tease people through their names, regardless of what their name is. For example, some names are humorously linked to their owner's functions. Think of some examples of "well-named" individuals, like Larry Speakes, former White House spokesman, or Dr. Henry Bone, osteoporosis specialist in Detroit.

Some cultural groups have great creativity in wordplay teasing over names. In some African-American cultural groups, for example, members especially young men, "play the dozens," competing to see who can insult the other most creatively. In Britain, some lower-class groups have been wonderfully creative with wordplay, and much Cockney-rhyming slang involves manipulating names. Can you think of examples of playing on names in your own lives? ◀

▶ *Write Now! What About Nicknames?*

Write a journal entry about nicknames you have been called throughout your life. Who called you what? How did they make you feel, and why? If you never had a nickname, did you always want one? What nickname did you want? What nicknames do you call yourself in your interior speech? Are they funny? Positive? Derogatory? Do a 10-minute free-write on your reflections. ◀

Words, Names, Meanings

> *A name, like a face, is something you have when you're not alone.*
>
> *—Dillard, 1977*

But how do words or names (not all words are names, of course) come to have meaning in the first place? In Plato's dialogue *Cratylus* (fifth century B.C.E.), Socrates explores this issue. One argument was that words are social conventions, signs that people agree on socially for convenience. (The term *tree*, agreed upon by English speakers, is arbitrary, as is proved by the fact that in French, speakers designate the same object as *arbre*.) The second argument was that names are "motivated" by the essentials of the thing itself: There must be something "tree-like" about a tree. Early on in human history, this magical language theory held sway, so that knowing something about the word T-I-G-E-R would give you knowledge of and control over the predator itself. This theory in Christianity came from the Bible: Language was given to Adam (or to Adam and Eve) by God. Adam named the animals according to their essential natures. Thus, a tiger was a tiger because of its tigerness.

This "Adamic" view of language led to many things, such as the Kabbalists repeating and rearranging the names of God to reach spiritual knowledge, or alchemists playing with the word G-O-L-D in their efforts to create gold. By the Enlightenment, language scholars were beginning to think of language more as a convention, at the crossroads between the individual and social life. Yet there were still problematic words, such as onomatopoeic words or other sounds that seemed symbolic. As for Socrates, he never really made up his mind on language, although he leaned toward convention. Although words may stand for concepts, however, names usually stand for particular people. But names can be symbolic, too. Look at the names of the characters in a novel or play if you want to know something about the meaning of the tale. Names in literature are often motivated by and carry clues to the essence of the characters.

Moving from the "name" to the "signature," the authors of *Text Book* (Scholes et al., 1995) make a connection between language, naming, and music, bringing in the term *signature*. A signature is a sign in written music but it can also stand for a writing style, your fingerprint of language use, or how you sign your name. Many theories of how language began connect meaning with music and song, with tone of voice, sound, and rhythm.

▶ *Write and Design Now! Family Names and Coats of Arms*

Family names: What do you know about your family name? Do you know less about your mother's family name? Sometimes people change names as political or religious gestures. Names have also been altered, often simplified or Anglicized, by registrars at immigration points such as Ellis Island. Talk to family members. You may also need to look in the library at books on the history of names such as by Charles Berlitz. Many names are linked with professions, such as Miller or Smith, to places, like -*burg*, or to family relations, such as names ending with -*son*.

Visual thinking about names: In the medieval world, great families often had animals and other visual symbols of their heritage and lands displayed on shields divided into quadrants. These displays, called *coats of arms*, had a small shield replicating the most important family shield in the center, at the crossroads of the four quadrants. This was called "the abyss." It represented perpetuity, in the same way that reflecting mirrors reproduce an image in infinite regression.

Where do we find such heraldry in the modern world? Don't these function similarly to image-producing corporate logos? (A search of websites will yield both family crests and logos.)

Does your family have a family crest from heraldry with symbolic figures? If so, explicate the text and images in writing. If not, create one for yourself. Use your name and/or nickname(s). Most coats of arms had a family motto underneath the shield that explained or tied into the four images on the quadrants. Be sure to write such a motto. Puns were a central feature of these mottos. For example, the Bernard family's icon was a bear, and their motto was "Bear and forebear." ◀

▶ *Writing from Names*

Write an essay about your name—your entire name. This essay need not the "well-made box," as my former professor Winston Weathers has called the traditional essay (1980). Let yourself have a bit of fun. Try this process for writing an essay on your name:

1. Generate text by talking, brainstorming, listing, and freewriting about names and nicknames. Ask questions or do research as needed.

2. Extend the listing/freewriting: Make associations, spinoffs, comparisons, contrasts, analogies, silly puns, etc.

3. Think visually as well. Illustrate your ideas. You can use metaphors—intersections of two unlike things—which are interesting and usually visual. To play on my own name, Hobbs, for example, I found that a hob is a kind of nail. So as an older sister, I am like a nail in that I hold things—my siblings—together. I am also a hob because I am hard and can be driven.

4. Expand into narratives and descriptions. Comment on your name items as they are relevant to your life's experience.

5. Have a classmate or someone in your writer's group read your essay, using the following guidelines.

6. When you are finished, think about how the process of writing this essay relates to the process of writing in general. ◀

▶ *Guidelines—Reading the Naming Essay*

The following criteria are to guide you as you read early versions of the essays on names. You can use the points to evaluate your own writing or to comment on a group member's work:

Overall:

- Does the piece fit the assignment of being an experimental paper about names? Does the paper sound as if the writer has gotten into the spirit of the paper, has done some family research, had some fun with it? Are there important insights as well?

- Was the essay enjoyable to read? What impact did it have on you?
- Did the paper as a whole deliver on the promise the writer makes in the beginning? What bothers you at the end? If you are satisfied, what makes you satisfied?
- Did the writer meet his or her own goals and purposes in the paper?

Development:

- How does the writer develop the paper? Are there plenty of creative associations, details, and surprising and creative connections? Are there some good details?
- Is a personal history included?
- Does the paper reveal something about the person?
- Does the paper make sense to the reader? Would it make sense to any reader?

Organization:

- How does the paper flow? Can the reader follow it?
- If there is a jazz-like organization, can it be improved, or is it enjoyable the way it is? Can the paper be made even more interesting by being more experimental?

Style (choice of words, shape of sentences, affecting tone, flavor, voice):

- Is there variety of expression?
- Is there creativity?
- Does the paper use specific language? Concrete and picturesque language?
- Does the writer use effective sentence patterns for this paper?

Conventions: (grammar and mechanics):

- Is the grammar appropriate to the writer's purpose?
- How about places where the writer fails to use conventions of standard written English? How should these be judged in this piece? Do the experiments work or not?

The following student examples may not be particularly experimental structurally. Nonetheless, they show you some insights other students have arrived at by reflecting on their names. Discuss how they made use of this assignment to arrive at self-understanding.

Bonner Jack Slayton

"Is This Who I Am?"

> *Life goes on . . .*
> *The dead be forgotten*
> *Life goes on . . .*
> *Though good men die*
> *Life goes on . . .*
> *I forget just why*
> *Lament*
>
> *—Edna St. Vincent Millay*

Life goes on. It must pass from generation to generation. This history unfolds in my name—Bonner Jack Slayton. Each name is distinct, each having a history establishing a definition of who I am and where I have come from.

Bonner, an historical last name used first. It is a name which has caused much embarrassment to me. Parents have ridiculed me over it. It is always mispronounced and has always been misprinted (I had to return my high school diploma because of this). Yet it wasn't until I searched for the history of my name that I realized its importance to me as a person.

It comes from the Deep South. I am named after my great grandmother on my mother's side—Vinnie Bonner. She was an amazing woman. Born in 1902, her life spanned 14 presidents, two world wars, the Great Depression, the automobile and the space shuttle. Her life was as exciting as her life span. Her grandparents owned slaves and her grandfather fought for the Confederacy. She grew up in a South which was being Reconstructed. She grew up with the children and grandchildren of slaves. Her life was poor, but the history which it covered was awesome.

Jack—a middle name coming from my father. It spans five generations (now six), each the first born, each male and each having the middle name as Jack. "ASDF", Arville, Bobby,

Larry, Bonner and now Kaleb. Each generation responsible for carrying on the family history. This name is from the Midwest and ultimately from the Mother country—Germany.

Again a war, even two. My ancestors are from a country which twice tried to conquer the world. Can there be any pride in this? A question I must ask in order for my life to go on. As with the Civil War, some of my family fought on the losing side.

Slayton—my last name. Again, a history is passed on. Yes this name also includes a war, not a world war, but you might say a civil war. My great grandfather and his father had a war. Arville decided it was time to leave the Midwest. He took the name, subtracted a letter and added two more. "Slaten" it had been, but history can be changed, especially when you move to a new place, a place called Oklahoma.

Vinnie remembers being a part of another war. The Simms War it was called. A family feud that left many dead and many hurt in the backwoods of Mississippi and Alabama. Bill Simms and John Bonner had fought in the Civil War together. When they got out, they came to blows. My great grandmother remembered. She was tossed out of a wagon as a little girl. She hid behind a fallen tree trunk one time—it was the only thing that saved her life.

Conflict and war. It is woven throughout my name.

This next student combined her birth writing with writing about her name:

Kelsey Marie Martyn-Farewell

"What's in a Name"

In my search for information on my name and how I came to have it, I started to become interested in more of my family's genealogy, a project that grows larger every day. A few simple questions about my name started me on the fascinating trail to discover my roots. But it all started with my own name, Kelsey Marie Martyn-Farewell.

I was born on August 11, 1981 at the Topeka Holistic Birth and Growth Center at 8:10pm. My parents were always quick to point out that I was born with a full head of jet-black hair, including bangs and hair already going down my neck, as well as having been very active since my time in the womb. My mother joked that it took her more time to recover from her bruised ribs from the pregnancy, a full six weeks, than it did to recover from her grueling labor.

As it happened, my birth was overdue. Not that my delay in any way kept my mom stuck at home; she worked, sometimes barefoot, in the hospital as a social worker until a few days before I was born. About eight days after my expected due date, Dr. Jessie stripped my mother's membrane to help induce labor in the next few days. And it worked. Two days later my mom awoke in the middle of the night to the beginnings of her labor. She decided, however, to go back to bed, and she slept the rest of the night. But in the morning she and dad packed up the car with all of the soon-needed baby gear and drove from their home in Lawrence to Topeka, where the Center was located.

"To go off as two people and come back as three. I still shake my head. It was really weird. We kept thinking, 'What have we done?!?' "

My parents arrived at the Center in the morning of the 11th, much too early as they discovered since I wasn't born until after eight o'clock that evening. Like many first childbirths, my mom's labor was long—over 15 hours. In fact, she lost her steam near the end of her labor. Mom still thanks her midwife, Ginger, for just being there and possessing so much energy that she shared with my mom. Ginger's energy alone was not enough, though, so Dr. Jessie and Ginger fed mom spoonfuls of honey for that little extra boost. They feared that my mother would pass out from exhaustion and not be able to deliver the baby naturally.

Sure enough, that little extra energy helped my mom to successfully deliver an eight pound baby girl. The only people mom remembers calling after the birth were her parents, who lived only a few hours away. My family chuckled at the announcement since my mom had two sisters, no brothers, and here came another female to add to the list. Of course, I was the first grandchild only on that side of the family. My mother was later redeemed when she had the first boy of her family, my brother, four and a half years later.

As I had taken my time being born, my family and I spent the night at the Center. The next morning I had my first visitor,

Dr. Jessie's mom, not my grandparents, much to their dismay. It was especially heart-wrenching for my grandmother because she and Dr. Jessie's mom had known each other for years, and it just wasn't fair that she should see the new grandbaby first! After the visit, we packed up the car again to head home to Lawrence. The Center was so kind as to give me a little gray tee-shirt to sport home along with my oh-so-fashionable diaper. Any more clothes and I would have suffocated in the hot August sun. We soon arrived at our little blue house on Illinois Street to start the rest of our lives together.

My parents chose not to find out my gender until my birth, but they had a name picked out for each gender. My mother, while she was pregnant, kept a list of baby names she liked with her at all times, just in case she found another one she liked. As soon as they discovered I was a girl, they were eager to give me a name.

My first name, Kelsey was the last name of an actress, Linda Kelsey, and my mom really liked the idea of Kelsey as a first name; she thought it would be unique. My mom also claims that she got a "strong sense" from that name, and the rest was history. Kelsey was historically a last name, but in the past century has become a more popular first name. If it came from Old Norse, it meant from "Ship Island," but "ship victory" from Old English.

My middle name, Marie, as it turns out, is not legally my middle name. Upon investigation on how I got my first name I discovered that I was born without a middle name at all. My Birth Certificate reads: Kelsey Martyn-Farewell. It wasn't until my brother's birth four and a half years later, Hamilton, that my parents gave any thought into a middle name for me. My brother got the middle name Ray, which was my father's father's name. So my mother thought it would be appropriate if I shared a middle name with my father's mother. Apparently when the decision to add Marie to my name, my parents started the paperwork but never went through with it. So it seems that I haven't really had a middle name for the last sixteen years that I've claimed one!

Through another funny story I have also been called "Kelsey Beth" by my step-father, Wiley. He grew up in north Texas and Oklahoma and likes to call people by their first and middle names. I guess he never bothered to ask what my middle name was, he just assumed I might as well be a "Kelsey Beth." Well, when I was fifteen and taking driver's ed one summer, 'Beth' became more officially a part of my name. When you finish driver's ed, they give you this green little business-like card stating your full name and that you completed driver's ed for your insurance companies. Upon my completion of the program, I picked up my prize of the little green card, only instead of Marie, Beth appeared as my middle name.

I went to the office to clear the matter up. I couldn't have just any name on my prize, I wanted my *real* name! I took my complaint to the secretary. I explained the situation to her in full and asked how this random name came to appear as my own. Her only suggestion was that if my middle name wasn't listed on my registration for the course, they probably called home to get it. (Why they just didn't ask me, who knows?)

Ah-ha! Obviously they got Wiley on the phone, and instead of just admitting that he didn't know my middle name, he told the secretary that it was Beth. The secretary, who was eager to return to her daily tasks, told me that it didn't really matter what middle name the card said at all. The only people to see it were the insurance agents, and she was confident that they could figure out the mystery of my middle names. I couldn't wait to rush home and ask him about it.

When I asked Wiley about the misnomer of the day, he just laughed and admitted to the whole thing. He could only remember calling me "Kelsey Beth," so he couldn't recall my real name.

I didn't get the whole story on this strange "Marie" middle name incident until several months after I found out it wasn't legally my middle name. My mother was very reluctant to talk about it and was still very hurt by the situation, seventeen years later. Apparently, my father's parents didn't know that my mother had hyphenated her name when she married my dad. So, when I was born, they assumed that Martyn was my middle name, a trait I've found to be very common with my ancestors.

When Hamilton was born "Hamilton Ray Martyn-Farewell" they started to get a clue that Martyn was not a middle name. My parents wanted to give me Alpha's middle name when my brother was born, but my grandparents apparently hit the ceiling. They said things to my mother that she will not repeat to this day, even though they have both died years ago. My grandparents were so taken aback that it took them three months after my brother's birth to come and visit him.

I hope to find out through my genealogy research if Marie has been a family name, or if it started with Alpha. So far I have found several "Mary"s, but only Alpha has claimed "Marie."

My last name also has a bizarre history. When my parents married, my mom hyphenated her maiden name, Marial Martyn, to add my father's family name, Farewell. When my mom got pregnant with me, their first child, they decided to give the double whammy to their children as well. Of course, eight years after I was born my parents divorced and my mom dropped Farewell from her name. My brother and I, however, were stuck with the hyphen.

I have asked if there was a lot of discussion about giving the kids the double last name, as has my brother. Although my dad didn't have Martyn as a part of his name, my mother convinced him that since the children were a part of them both, that they should get both last names.

I didn't understand this until recent years. Throughout my elementary and middle school years I battled with my name. I used to pick one last name or the other to write on my homework assignments. I would also go through all the possible combinations of my four names to see which one was really *mine*. I didn't know anyone else (until later years in life) who had a hyphenated name, so I thought about legally changing my name to just one last name.

It wasn't until high school that I started to realize that the hyphenated name was my *true* name. (Whether it was more *true* because I could never decide which name to pick, I'll never know.) By true I mean that it fit with who I thought I was and made me a unique person in a sea of single last named people. Upon that realization I also came to the conclusion that, if I were ever to marry, I did not want to change my name. I had grown attached to the hyphen in my process of trying to get rid of it. The hyphen somehow morphed from a bothersome hand cramp to the name by which I defined myself. However, I didn't want to pain my future children with a triple last name, as much as those around me joked about it. ("Even better, you could marry someone who already has a hyphenated name! Then your kids could have all four!") So, my kids could take their father's name and I could keep mine.

This way everyone would have his or her identity intact. By everyone, I of course, mean me.

Names tell a lot about a person. My genealogy research into my mother's side of the family has proved fruitful already. I can trace back to the first Martyn from the Waldsmith family, who came to the United States in the late 1700s to start a mission. That first Waldschmidt (spelling changed later) had a granddaughter who had three children by two different men. She was never married, something very scandalous for her time. It was the last of her three children, Peter Waldsmith Martyn, who passed the Martyn name through the family tree. Nothing is known about his father, so further Martyn ancestry remains a mystery. The name itself comes from "Martinus," the god of war.

Also on my mother's side are the Valentines (my grandmother's maiden name). The Valentines immigrated to America in the mid–1600s, starting off in New Jersey. Several doctors, reverends, writers, and judges came from this family. The history of the name comes from the Roman family name *Valentinus* which was from Latin *valens* "strong, vigorous, and healthy". Saint Valentine was a 3rd-century martyr. His feast day was the same as the Roman fertility festival of Lupercalia, which resulted in the association between Valentine's day and love.

From my father's side come the Farewells and the Pages. Farewell most likely comes from the saying "Farewell!" when leaving a room, while Page comes from an Old French surname which originally denoted a person who was a page to a lord. My interest in cooking lies somewhere in my father's side of the family. My grandparents, Ray and Alpha, were always cooking something, it seemed, and passed a love of food on to my brother and me.

Something that didn't surprise me at all was that more information was known by more people in my family about our matrilineage. This was mainly because the research into family lineage was done by women, not men. I think, also, that women are more prone these days to keeping track of their lineage and the important women in their heritage. This is made even more apparent on my mom's side of the family, where my grandmother had three daughters and no sons.

This search I've begun on my meaning as a person through the genealogy of my family has become quite the addiction. Somewhere between the idea that people have traits related to their names and the fascination of family history, I have started a life-long project of research. My goal has become to compile all the family history for both sides and supplement it with little biographies with the important and interesting people in my family.

But all this genealogy is just finding names on a sheet of paper, isn't it? So, what's in a name? For me it tells a lot. It is a reminder of my early years' trials and battle for an identity. As of this moment, I don't have a legal middle name, but I've claimed "Marie" as my own for so long that it has become a part of who I think I am. (In fact, it appears on my Social Security card.) Whether I ever go to the extent to add it legally, I don't know. I do know that Kelsey Marie Martyn-Farewell is who I am, and who I will continue to be.◄

► *Write Now! Your Name, an Acrostic Poem*

Here is another trick with names, from Wendy Bishop and Melanie Rawls (2000, 24–25):

- List all the letters in your name, but mix them up. Do leave the last letter the same.
- Work your name/nickname out so it is between 8 and 14 letters.

For each letter, in turn, beginning with the first:

- Write a sentence with six words and a color, describing you.
- Write a reoccurring dream you've had or have.
- List several things, beginning with the same initial letter, that can be found in your room.
- Include something you regularly say, spoken words.
- Describe yourself (use physical attributes).
- Describe yourself (use habits).
- Describe yourself (include eyes, hair, or facial features).
- List your five favorite possessions.

- Describe yourself in your favorite clothes.
- Include something you're often found eating.
- Use a sentence with two dashes.
- Include nicknames you've liked or disliked.
- Tell something people can't tell from looking at you.
- Write a sentence with three or less words.
- Include animals or plants you like.
- Choose the words "but I never," "but I always," "someday I'll," "in the meantime," or any transition that helps close the poem. Add them to the second to the last letter line of your name.
- End with a truth or insight.

Then rearrange the lines so that your name, spelled in the right order, forms the initial letter of each line. Modify things to create movement between the lines.

Monica Guadelupe Gomez

"Acrostic"

Mirror, money, mountains,
Once again you disappoint me. Where does the dream end and reality begin?
No need for words, they are as useless as pointless. We don't need to
  speak, only to feel.
I will never make the same mistake twice, but I always do, and each time
  learn a new lesson.
Close your eyes.
Attitude, strong, unstoppable.
Grandpa's paintings, a gift from Tammy, a book of memories, a necklace,
  an old friend.
Under shadows, brown outlined in black, a freckled canvas.
Always waiting until tomorrow.
Dog, dude, pumpkin, sweetie.
Another tall, brown-eyed girl.
Look, red on brown, red on gray.
Under there—hurry.
Push, push me again, push as hard as you can, you will give up before I fall.
Everything you put out there comes back to you. ◀

Places and Names

Particular place names have resonances that can make your writing sing. As Judith Barrington (1997, 121) notes, "In some cases, the name itself carries layers of history and imagery more apt than any image the writer could add." Names may reveal a history of colonialization or immigration. They also add to the believability of a story, as well as the musicality of the text. The very name of the state where I live, Oklahoma, means "land of the red people." The state was Indian Territory until it was taken by whites in a series of land runs and lotteries in the late nineteenth century. Many of the towns have Indian names, such as Chickasha, Okemah, and Gotebo. Include in your writing particular details—such as names of streets, buildings, towns, rivers, and mountains—and explore the histories of these names to give yourself credibility as a writer and also to help yourself understand the geography of your memoirs.

▶ *Read and Write Now!*

Read the following memoir excerpts on place and analyze how the writers use details in their place memories and descriptions. Then write either your personal memories of a place or an objective description, or combine the two. The first piece is my own, while the second is from essayist Nicholas Howe's (2003) *Across an Inland Sea: Writing in Place from Buffalo to Berlin.*

Catherine Hobbs

"Panhandle Memories"

My first memories are of the bare and windswept plains of the Oklahoma Panhandle where I was born, in Guymon at a chiropractic clinic. At first we lived in a little house in Goodwell. The Panhandle could be extremely hot or cold. I remember one black cold night my little hand was in my father's safely larger mitt on the way home from Sunday evening services as we ran alongside a road, peering into a ditch along the way (I may have been the only one running). I remember a suffocatingly hot day at a religious encampment where we sang "Give me oil in my lamp, keep me burning." I recall the horned toads we played with near the canvas tents.

In Texoma, I remember playing endless hours with my older brother Steve, climbing around in the empty shell of a neighboring house—abandoned and falling down? New and just being built? I recall my brother's cutting my finger with a knife, and although no one else remembers, I do have a small, white scar on the inside of my right middle finger. I remember our red Irish setter dog Paddy, left behind with neighbors when we moved to central Oklahoma when I was four. I recall my brother and I throwing my father's ruffneck paddle onto the roof—actually, I recall our invisible playmates Nella and Dee-Dee's throwing the paddle.

I remember the family listening to an old black Emerson radio when I was small. One of my first visual memories is the clear red light that shone in the black radio; I may have been two or three. The radio played "Take me out to the ball game" and everyone sang along. I remember my fourth birthday when I got a little tin tea set. My five-year-old brother Steve told me over and over the day before, "We did NOT get you a tea set for your birthday!" I recall standing beside a rusty fence looking into the chicken yard next door and soiling my thick training panties, and how upset my young mother was to have to clean me up, making us late to church. I remember my father's enjoyment of playing baseball until he broke his thumb.

My brother and I spent the eternity of childhood riding tricycles in a deepening circle in our small fenced yard, swinging in our swings—except for the time the chicken blood got under the swing when Mom killed a chicken for dinner. I recall the smell of the pinfeathers she burnt off on the gas stove burner. I remember the dust storm that came in one evening and raged into the night, dust filtering in the cracks of the windows, filling up our jack-O-lantern, mother sweeping and sweeping, my parents shoveling the dust to get the car—a black Dodge coupe—out of the driveway.

I recall watering a carrot-top garden growing in white milkglass saucers in the front windows, sweeping the wooden floor, my young mother leading us in a plaintive chant of "Daddy, come hooome . . . " at the end of what may have been a long day with children and house. I remember getting out of bed to look at an owl the neighbors spotted in a tree between our houses (but I never really saw it). I recall my brother's waking me up in the middle of the night yelling, my parents searching our bedroom because he believed a cow was hiding in the closet. Our Panhandle days ended when my father took us to the middle of the pan where he would go to graduate school on the GI bill.

Nicholas Howe

"Openlands: Oklahoma"

In a transient land rich with stories of migration, history lies not in what is preserved artificially, such as the old barracks at Fort Sill where Geronimo and other Indian leaders of the 1890s were imprisoned, but in the abandoned farm-houses throughout the state that survive, windowless, to the wind and sun. These remains memorialize those who lived on the edge and could not weather the harsh life of Oklahoma. They were built to shelter those who came with visions of the promised land and then were either "tractored off" in Steinbeck's metaphor for the fate of sharecroppers and small farmers of the thirties, or were, in a hard time, simply forgotten. Around these abandoned farmsteads one typically finds a stand of trees planted when the house was built and that now marks it as the site of earlier settlement. These small groves break the flow of grain or cotton sweeping along to the horizon. The land of those who once lived in these houses has often been joined to the spreads of more successful neighbors, though success here may simply have meant having a bit more water. Abandoned farmhouses appear everywhere in the American landscape, but those in Oklahoma have entered the national imagination through the enduring black-and-white images of the Dust Bowl taken by Arthur Rothstein and the other Farm Security Agency photographers of the late thirties.

So it is with towns like the fabled Gotebo of southwest Oklahoma, the place that signifies "the middle of nowhere" or "the back of beyond" to central Oklahomans. Gotebo has a row of what were once fine stone-built stores that displayed a solid prosperity and testified to their builders' faith in the future. Now the storefronts have collapsed, the roofs cannot keep out the rain, and the stores are filled with rusting junk. A town built for the long haul collapsed within a generation or two. It seems an act of mercy that today the state highway skirts the town and leads drivers past newly built gas stations and convenience stores. . . .

The evidence of busted dreams lies along the sides of roads leading into and out of Oklahoma. . . . I photographed empty houses bleached to silver-gray by the sun; standing on the edge of enormous fields, they were quietly moving in their mute isolation. ◄

► *Write Now! The Importance of Place*

Novelist Rilla Askew, author of *The Mercy Seat, Fire in Beulah*, and other works set in Oklahoma, sometimes asks her fiction writing students to bring in a newspaper clipping that represents something to them about their part of the state. Then she asks them to make up a story about it, usually a fictional short story. But newspaper articles can also spark reminiscences for memoirs. Find a newspaper clipping that reminds you of something about a place that is significant to you. Then free-write in your journal, focusing on describing and revealing your emotions about the place. Show it to some readers, asking them what kind of feeling they get from the writing and what they learn about the writer. ◄

3

Crafting Life Narratives: Elements of Stories in Time

Every child born carries the legacy of both parents. That legacy includes more than twenty-three pairs of elaborate, chemically complex chromosomes. It also includes the history that shaped the lives of both parents. In my case, that history includes some of the more powerful undercurrents of the experiences of many African Americans during the final generation of slavery and the first generation of emancipation.

—Ada Lois Sipuel Fisher, 1996

Ada Lois Sipuel Fisher, born only one generation away from slavery, fought to become the first African American to attend the law school at the University of Oklahoma. She successfully challenged the state's segregation laws in 1946, gaining admission to the all-white school and going on to contribute as an educator and attorney throughout her long life. Perhaps you believe it is easier for such key players during times of significant upheaval to see themselves as embedded in history. We all live similarly in the broader stream of history, however, and your teachers and writing group members can help you reflect on your own historical positioning through the life-writing activities in this chapter and their responses to your writing.

Nothing works like experience and practice, so you should attempt to place your life in a wider context, to write at the boundaries of self and society, private and public worlds. Seeing your life this way can give you a different perspective and lead to insight and understanding. For that reason, this chapter, which continues to discuss inventional prompts for autobiographies and moves into elements of craft, begins with a project in research and writing.

Creating Timelines and Writing Our Lives

> *When we begin the task of transcribing our life into text—of writing our story—we move beyond the set stage and bear witness to the wider theatre of our life. We begin to view these scenes differently and to discern the pattern that connects them. We look back and then we look ahead, and in this sense, we become both actor and director of the part that is the rest of our life.*
> *—Irene Karpiak, 2001*

First we will create two timelines: one for what is usually called your "private" life and one for your "public" life. The interrelations between the two become the ground from which insights may spring.

▶ *Write Now! Making Timelines*

Make a timeline of key events in your personal life. Former Secretary General of the United Nations Dag Hammarskjöld titled his autobiography *Markings* and used images of major stepping stones, signposts, or flags in life history. What were the major events, encounters, or decisions in your family and your close-in life? What were your stepping stones?

Similarly, choose a book or website with timelines for key public events that occurred in your lifetime and just before. A *World Almanac* often comes in handy for such a task or just look up "timelines" on a web search engine or visit a public television website. When you are finished, sit down with both your private and public timelines and reflect: How did events in the wider world affect you? Can you see state or national events that influenced the direction of your life, however slightly? A bad economic period might have led to your going to one college rather than another, for example. Or perhaps a monumental event shook you personally along with everyone else.

I'm thinking here of the assassinations of President John F. Kennedy, Martin Luther King Jr., and Robert Kennedy when I was in my adolescence. Most people of my generation know exactly where they were when each of these events took place. My students of one generation all named the *Challenger* disaster as a milestone event. Many of them watched the launch in their elementary classrooms, horrified when the teacher onboard was killed before their eyes. In Oklahoma, my students write about the bombing of the Murrah Federal Building in Oklahoma City. My present and future students will no doubt write about the September 11, 2001, plane crash destruction of the World Trade Center twin towers.

- Talk over these things with your writing group members. Often in writing classes when I give this assignment, students of the same generations find that similar events affected them but often in different ways.

- Write a reflection on the impact of an event in your life, your response or lack of response to events, your lack of awareness of events, or whatever connection you find between the personal and wider world timelines. You may choose to keep various timelines—perhaps political events, popular or high culture, key public figures, or whatever is meaningful to you as representing a wider culture or public world.

- Chaos theory proposes that even a seemingly slight event, such as the flap of a butterfly's wing in Venezuela, can have a major impact. The slight puff of air in South America may interact with a complex of weather systems to cause a storm in North America. Can you detect any slight shifts in your life that produced similar major effects?

Timeline of Catherine Lynn Hobbs

These events from my life are mostly public, but there are a few personal milestones thrown in for good measure.

- '50s and '60s, general climate: Besides the Korean War, there was much dangerous conflict and tension between the U.S.S.R. and U.S., giving way to an official detente. Tension with China exists throughout the era. The breakdown of 19th- and early 20th-century colonial systems gave rise to higher prices for raw materials. Economically, this period contributed to the inflation of the '70s.

- 1951, my birth year, Guymon, OK. Peace was made with Japan. Pres. Truman relieves MacArthur. Other major leaders include Mao Zedong in China, Stalin in the Soviet Union, and George V, father of Elizabeth, in Great Britain.
- LeCorbusier designs skyscrapers.
- 1952-H-Bomb exploded.
- 1953-Structure of DNA revealed.
- 1954-McCarthy censured, ending a reign of paranoia concerning Reds.
- 1954-*Brown vs. the Board of Education*, Supreme Court rules against segregation.
- 1953–55-Polio vaccine invented and administered.
- 1955-Geneva Conference divides Vietnam into North and South after communist victories.
- 1955-Computers invented; by 1960 they are in use.
- 1954–55-Warsaw Pact unites Soviets.
- 1955-Rosa Parks refuses to give up her seat on a bus in Montgomery, Alabama.
- 1957-Chomsky theorizes grammatical speech is in part a function of biology and development of the brain.
- 1957-Russia launches *Sputnik I* satellite.
- 1958-U.S. launches Explorer I and the space race.
- 1958-National Defense in Education Act boosts funding for sciences, also English.
- 1958-Stereophonic records begin.
- 1959-Castro in Cuba.
- 1960-Civil Rights Act focuses on voting by African Americans.
- 1960-Integrated circuits are miniaturizing.
- 1961-Berlin Wall is built.
- 1961-Bay of Pigs invasion of Cuba by U.S., Peace Corps founded.

- 1961-First manned space flight by Soviets.
- 1961-Telstar, first communication satellite, launches.
- 1963-Nuclear Test Ban treaty.
- 1963-JFK ASSASSINATED.
- 1964-BEATLES come to U.S.
- 1964-China explores bomb.
- 1964–68-Military buildup in the West.
- 1965-Johnson orders Vietnam bombing; march from Selma led by King leads to new Voting Rights Act.
- 1967-I have DeJuana Jones as an English teacher at Norman High School.
- 1968-MARTIN LUTHER KING SHOT.
- 1968-ROBERT KENNEDY SHOT.
- 1968-Student revolt in Paris.
- 1969-Neil Armstrong walks on Moon, arrives in Apollo 11.
- 1969-Woodstock, years of disillusion with NHS.
- 1969–70-Finishing the summer Revolutionary Intensive Learning Program at OU, I go to Oklahoma College of Liberal Arts in Chickasha.
- 1970-Kent State killings of war protesters by National Guardsmen.
- 1972-Passing of Equal Rights Amendment, never ratified by states.
- 1973-I graduate from OU with a degree in journalism, while WATERGATE looms. I get my first newspaper job.
- 1973-U.S. Troops leave Vietnam.
- 1973-Oil shortage, prices up, inflation. I buy my first car, a Toyota Corolla.
- 1975-I get married, leave my second and final newspaper job, move to Louisville.
- 1976-Bicentennial.
- 1976-Mao Zedong dies.
- 1976-Women admitted to Episcopal priesthood.
- 1978-Spain establishes constitutional monarchy.
- 1979-Khomeini rises to power.
- 1979–81-hostages held in Iran.

- 1978-First test tube baby born in England, Louise Brown.
- 1978-I return from six months in Europe riding mopeds to settle in Tulsa.
- 1979-Smallpox "eradicated."
- 1980-Rise of conservative Moral Majority.
- 1980-Soviet invasion of Afghanistan spurs U.S. pullout from Moscow Olympics.
- 1980-John Lennon shot and killed.
- 1981-First woman Supreme Court judge named.
- 1982-AIDS getting attention for the first time.
- 1982-Oil glut, Vietnam Memorial dedication.
- 1983-I get my Master's from Tulsa University.
- 1985-I leave Oklahoma to study at Purdue; 8.1 earthquake in Mexico, sister Jeannie there for honeymoon rushes out of her hotel.
- 1987-Stock market plunge.
- 1989-Glass pyramid added to the Louvre in commemoration of the bicentennial of the French Revolution.
- 1989-San Francisco Bay earthquake.
- 1989-I receive my Ph.D. degree from Purdue University, go to Illinois State University.
- 1992-I move back to Norman to teach at Oklahoma University.
- 1994-I am divorced, receive tenure, buy my first house. America is finally declared polio free.
- 1995-Murrah Federal Building in OKC bombed.
- 1995-I publish edited collection *Nineteenth-Century Women Learn to Write*.
- 1999-Sabbatical year, six months in Europe; Mom gets colon cancer but survives.
- 2001-Publish *Rhetoric on the Margins of Modernity*.
- 2001-World Trade Center towers fall.
- 2002-My friend Mark moves to my town.
- 2003-U.S. invades Iraq.
- 2004-Post-war occupation, world terrorism, economy uncertain.

In reflecting on my timeline, I found that I could and perhaps should write a memoir about growing up as a girl in
the so-called "Heartland" in the Cold War period, something
I have never written about. Also, I noticed several historical
events that shaped my life—one before my lifetime, the GI
bill, and one in my childhood, the National Defense in
Education Act, which I learned pumped money into the
schools in both the sciences and in English during the Race for
Space after the Soviets beat us into space with *Sputnik*. (I still
recall the two-inch newspaper headlines from the day *Sputnik*
was launched.) The social turmoil of the Vietnam War, the
Civil Rights movement, and the climate of Watergate all
moved me toward my first career in journalism. I still wonder
what effect it had on my personality to grow up in the turbu-
lent and traumatic era that was the '60s and '70s. People's
reactions to each era's events differ—depressed, I thought the
world was falling apart, while one of my peers optimistically
believed the terrible events were the final disruptions before a
revolution in which everything would be set aright.

My students have and will continue to face similar evaluation
and questioning after the World Trade Center bombings and their
aftermath. The 9/11 event of 2001 had a measure of influence on my life,
as it brought a friend who became my partner back to his hometown
to be closer to his family. My life contains many wider influences yet
than I have taken into account. My families' religious and Southern
heritage, the mixed attitudes to capitalism I received growing up in a
populist, Progressive Era state, the intellectual exercise of arguing with my
father, and my being reared by a stay-at-home mom during the era of
Betty Friedan's *The Feminine Mystique* also come to mind. ◀

▶ *Write Now! Discussing and Expanding Upon Timelines*

1. What phases and themes can you see in your chronologies? Choose
from your personal chronology no more than 8 to 12 key events. Write
about a few of the major milestones in your journal. What were the significant events, encounters, or decisions in your life, and why did you choose
these? Allow yourself to write freely again on another day. Did you change

the milestones? Can you identify phases or periods between milestones or after significant events?

2. Write about possible phases or themes as movements in your life, as in a symphony. How does one follow, expand upon, and turn from the one before? Here are other ideas inspired by a guide to journal-writing:

- Restlessness and boredom: Write about times you did not feel fully engaged in life.

- What is your work? Think about the work you have done at various times in your life—at school, in the workplace, or in your quest for your life's work or career.

- Who provides your models of behavior? After whom have you patterned your behavior and why?

- What moves you? What movies, music, friendships, art, or activities have made a positive or negative impact on you?

- Movement from dependence to independence: What phases of your life can you identify in the movement to independence?

- What other movements have you experienced? ◀

Examples of Students Working from Timelines:

Here is the opening segment of a student essay making use of her chronology:

> Twenty-one years ago, I was born in a small town named Morenci. The town today looks like a storybook ghost town. I go back occasionally to visit my dad. The town was once vibrant with the families of the miners who worked at the copper mine, my dad being one of them. It was 1981, and a new era of pop culture had just begun. The first IBM computers rolled off the lines, MTV made its debut, and a mysterious disease known at first for killing homosexuals was found to have the capability of affecting anyone—oh, and who can forget PacMan? Although these events did not seem to have an effect on my life at the time, they are pieces of a past that makes up the present.

When I was around the age of two, the miners in Morenci went on strike. The mine was not paying the workers what they deserved. While the strike was going on, Bruce Springsteen opened a free clinic for miners and their families. Springsteen was a huge celebrity back in those days and so it was a big deal. We were fortunate that he did that. After I turned three, my parents decided it would be best if we rooted ourselves in another city, and so off we went to make our home in Lawton, Oklahoma, where my grandparents lived . . . They lived there because my grandfather had been stationed at Ft. Sill, a military base that was formerly an Indian fort in the west . . .

How has this student used the events of her life to understand patterns in her life? How could she continue to trace their influence in her essay? Following that are further examples of papers written about significant milestone events. What meaning has Tara drawn from the events? How does metaphor help add to the atmosphere of the piece? Kevin's essay focuses on the impact of a single national event. Write a similar journal entry about a single milestone event, even if it is not as dramatic as the one here.

Tara Stine

"World Events and My Life"

Like many Americans, I live in a metaphoric bubble. My own little joys and sorrows comprise my world and fill my every thought. The amount of homework I am assigned or the smile of a guy in literature class defines current events, not a policy enactment in a distant nation. The fact that this creature of tunnel vision is somewhat affected by world events seems obvious. Yet the ways in which those events affect me—the subtle changes they exact upon my life—are interwoven with my existence in an almost imperceptible manner.

World War II, in which I certainly did not participate, and the Cold War, of which I learned long after its end, both indirectly developed my personality. Because of strained foreign relations, my military father and his new family were stationed in southern Germany. At a tender age I learned of the beauty of foreign voices, experienced tastes and weather patterns that I will never know again, and gaped in amazement at works of art that predate my homeland by centuries. The truest irony of this life is that the wholesome, American fear of "those vile Reds" actually gave me an open mind. The currently expanding U.S. economy has given me a comfortable life and, more importantly, allowed for immeasurable advances in medical technologies. These advances saved my young life from pneumonia in 1981 and diagnosed my grandmother with terminal cancer in 2000. The country's prosperity helped me live to know the feeling of helplessness in the face of inevitable death.

Smaller, more humorous memories carry the imprints of the world as well. The invention of the cell phone in 1983 allowed me to be caught with one in Pre-Calculus and sent to in-school restriction. The tornado of 1999 made the value of a new, only minutely dented Camaro decline into my father's price range. El Niño developed a cloud that created the small puddle in which that Camaro spun out on my graduation night.

So. O.J. Simpson never jaded my view of the legal system, nor did a Serbian refugee change my dietary habits. Still, my contracted world proves itself a bubble that would not exist without the vast pond upon which it floats.

Kevin Fischer

Milestone Journal-Writing: "Timeline Event"

My parents were still married when I was seven years old. I vividly remember that January day, the first day I remember seeing a spaceship going into space. This day the spaceship *Challenger* was to take seven people, including a school-teacher, into space.

You ask why this day was such a defining moment in my life? I can vividly remember lying on the couch, staying home because of illness, or faking it so I could see the shuttle take off and not have to miss a minute. I was eating saltine crackers and drinking Sprite, a ritual for any member of our family who didn't feel up to par. The room was dark, and the couch a cold fake leather texture. I watched intently as the news reporters talked about everything from the weather to Christa McAuliffe, a high school teacher from New Hampshire who was aboard the shuttle. Time seemed to move in slow motion. I just wanted to see the ship take off, just like every other kid my age.

The time was nearing, and I was on the edge of my seat but still able to act sick if Mother entered the room. The clock was ticking down, and the camera was affixed to the shuttle. I had heard all there was from reporters and seen all their graphs of preflight routines. I just imagined the astronauts in my head, strapping themselves down for the ride of their life. The clock hit zero, and the engines took off, the shuttle lifting off the ground like a ghost in a movie. Everything looked to be going just fine at Kennedy Space Center when 73 seconds into the making of history, tragedy hit. The shuttle began to spin out of control and smoke circled in the air. My life came to a halt; I had never witnessed such tragedy in my short life. To make the situation even more confusing, I had seen death on television before, but I was always told that it was fake, just a movie. This on the other hand wasn't fake; I had just witnessed seven people die like so many others that day. My mother held me and tried to console me. It was just a situation everyone had to face.

The moment changed my life forever; it made me less receptive and caring for others. How was I to react, with so many emotions flowing through my head? The way I chose to react to this tragedy was to act like it didn't happen and move on with my life. I attribute to this the way I handle most situations in my life—by acting like they didn't happen and just moving on with life.

> *Human life itself may be almost pure chaos, but the work of the artist . . . is to take these handfuls of confusion and disparate things . . . and put them together in a frame to give them some kind of shape and meaning.*
> —*Katherine Anne Porter*

The timeline assignments are designed to help you organize your life as well as to provide and help you understand possible events and phases that can be used to help frame essays or provide structure for beginning to write. Perhaps you want to recast your five chapters now. Or if you didn't propose a five-chapter autobiography, you now see how you would do it.

Crafting Autobiographical Narratives: Themes and Phases

> *My fatal weakness for standing aside from whatever was happening around me and translating it into vignettes of drama overcame me once more. . . . Unresisting, I let it assemble and take shape in my mind.*
>
> —Moss Hart, Act One, 1976

At this point, you should have a chronological list of selected major events of your outer, public world and another for your personal life. Displaying the most significant milestones visually on a timeline is a good starting point for various crossings and comparisons, and you should take some time to reflect on and incubate what you can discover about your marker dates. One thing to muse over is how to divide the timeline into shorter portions. That is, you should look for phases of your life, or themes in your life. These may have various time spans: A phase as you define it may last over several long periods of your life or may confine itself to one short period. A theme may, like a little musical melody, run through your life as a whole or may simply be there at a key point in your life and then dissipate. Perhaps you see a link between two disparate life events, so that, like two ends of a rainbow, they connect two points on your timeline. Take some time to reflect on possible themes or phases. Autobiographical writing can often be considered artful and well crafted not by how much goes into it but by what is left out, giving your writing focus. Allowing yourself enough time to reflect will pay off in the quality of your insights and your essay.

James Baldwin's (1962) *The Fire Next Time*, for example, contains an essay "Down at the Cross, letter from a region in my mind." It begins, "I underwent, during the summer that I became fourteen, a prolonged religious crisis" (27). It ends by describing and reflecting upon a meeting with the Nation of Islam leader Elijah Muhammad, told from the narrator's time, "When I was in Chicago last summer." The theme of this lengthy phase, covering much of Baldwin's adult life, was race and religion. In his autobiographical letter, Baldwin explores his personal religious history, trying to make sense of why he could not accept the

Black Muslim life offered by Elijah Muhammad and his followers. He once again reiterates the guiding insight of his life—that to hate white people would destroy him, as it had his father.

Scene and Summary in Autobiographical Writing

Memoirist Judith Barrington (1997) describes the structural elements of scene and summary in autobiographical pieces in visual, cinematic terms (81–82). A summary section is like a long shot, setting up the shot and orienting the reader. Generalizations are made, so that the reader will understand what's going on. Then a scene zooms in on a particular moment or event, providing a close-up shot. Summary often provides some "telling," in an effort to help the reader get his or her bearings. It can telescope time, allowing the writer to compress long periods of time into perhaps one long paragraph. A scene thus allows the reader to experience an event imaginatively, watching and even listening to dialog the writer has reconstructed as accurately as possible. The focus of a scene is tighter—thus less is seen—but what *is* seen is in perfect focus, so scenes carry particular sensory details: descriptions of sounds, visual objects, textures, temperatures, space, and light. Many memoirs, such as Baldwin's *The Fire Next Time*, contain much more summary than scene, only giving us the tight shot when we need to be "on the scene" to understand, such as moments in the conversation before and during a dinner with Elijah Muhammad.

Reflecting or Musing

Barrington often refers to the narrator's written reflections as "musings," and so they are. Perhaps the term *reflection* is too philosophical and heavy-handed for a memoir. Barrington calls musing "speculating about the facts," linking it with "the process of judging." Note, also, her warning: "Musing on what *might* have been behind that old photograph of your grandmother, or telling the reader how you've always *imagined* your parents' early lives, is not the same as presenting your speculations as facts." Many memoirs also follow this pattern: They carry summaries, interspersed with scenes, to tell a story. The story is then followed by musings or reflections on what the story might mean for the writer, who is seeking insight into the truth of his or her life. Barrington says:

> The memoirist need not necessarily know what she thinks about her subject but she must be trying to find out; she may never arrive at a definitive verdict, but she must be willing to share her intellectual and emotional quest for answers. . . . Self-revelation without analysis or understanding becomes merely an embarrassment to both reader and writer. (28–29)

After the scene of meeting with Elijah Muhammad, Baldwin reflects on historical relations between blacks and whites in the United States and the terrible suffering of blacks from "gratuitous violence" by whites. Then, reflecting on the beauty of black people, he writes:

> And when I sat at Elijah's table and watched the baby, the women, and the men, and we talked about God's—or Allah's—vengeance, I wondered, when that vengeance was achieved, *What will happen to all that beauty then?* I could also see that the intransigence and ignorance of the white world might make that vengeance inevitable . . . based on the law that we recognize when we say, "Whatever goes up must come down."
> . . . If we—and now I mean the relatively conscious whites and the relatively conscious blacks, who must, like lovers, insist on, or create, the consciousness of the others—do not falter in our duty now, we may be able, handful that we are, to end the racial nightmare, and achieve our country, and change the history of the world. If we do not now dare everything, the fulfillment of that prophecy, recreated from the Bible in a song by a slave, is upon us: God gave Noah the rainbow sign, No more water, the fire next time! (140–41)

Sometimes stories or series of stories really do (or should) speak for themselves, but not often. The kind of reflection and evaluation of events done here by James Baldwin exemplifies the writer's mind as it judges and presents the results of that judgment. The judgment is most often a probable one, for as human beings, we seldom have the whole truth. We seek to start a conversation, not have the last word. In auto-biographical writing, authors frequently use such reflective thought in their journey to craft a truth larger than their particular stories.

Elements of Narration in Time

As you probably know, the "hero" or "heroine" of a novel is called the *protagonist* in technical literary vocabulary. When you write memoir, your text not only has a protagonist, but it also has a narrator. Both are textual representations of *parts* of yourself at particular moments of your life. Memoirist Barrington (1997, 23) advises apprentice writers to "always refer to the character who is you in the story as 'the narrator;' not as 'I.'" Similarly, your colleagues and writing group members should refer to the protagonist of your story as "the narrator," not as "you." This allows you to get a bit of distance from your writing after you have drafted your work and are in the process of receiving feedback on it. It also keeps your group members from confusing you with the text you have written about your life and makes it easier for you to take criticism. After all, they are criticizing the work you have crafted for the purpose of making it better, not criticizing your life!

As a narrator, you generally speak from a particular point on your timeline about an earlier point on the line or a phase. Frequently you are writing retrospectively from a point of "now," as a more mature person writing about a less mature person at a particular point. Problems arise when you don't make this clear to readers or you confuse them with where you are in the story at a given point. Barrington advises students to diagram the time signals given in their stories on a story timeline, to make it perfectly clear to readers trying to follow a story what time they are in at any particular point in the narrative. Representing time is complex, and readers are frequently confused by autobiographical time.

There are many ways to tell a story, and although your timeline may lay out events one right after the other, telling most stories in this way might result in a cumbersome, forced march through time. As we have seen, Baldwin uses chronology to lead us from his 14-year-old religious self to his present spiritual views. His frequent use of summary collapses time in the early years and leaves gaps we might question.

As we focus our stories on our theme or phase, it is often preferable to begin the tale at a dramatic or essential point in the story, rather than *ab ovo*, or "from the egg" or origin. When we begin in the middle, however, it becomes necessary to construct flashbacks, as are used in most movies and novels, to fill in missing information. We may even want to have flash-forwards. All are permitted, as long as we are clear about where we are in time and send clear enough signals to readers. In experimental pieces, all rules are off (once you know them enough to know you are dispensing with them), but readers must still be able to construct a story for themselves from clues, however fragmented.

Most often, narrators will speak from a point close to the NOW and look back, using past tenses (most often formed with *–ed*). Present tense can also be used and has been trendy of late. However, this makes it more difficult for readers to sort out where they are in time, as present tense writing has even fewer cues for them to hang onto.

Recognizing Arrangements in Time

When you read a memoir or autobiography analytically, you learn a lot about how to work with time and narratives. In *Reading Autobiography*, Smith and Watson (2001, 170–71) advise that you pay attention to time and narration with questions like these:

- What is the "time of the telling"?
- At what stage of life does the narrator tell the tale? Publish the work?
- Does the narrator write about the actual telling of the tale, the "scene of writing"?
- Is there one moment of the telling, or are there several, with the author letting you know at various points that he or she has moved in the time of the telling?
- How are past, present, and future presented and organized in the story?
- Does the narrator begin at the beginning and tell the story continuously or begin in the middle and use flashbacks? What about flashforwards?
- Are there gaps in narration? How do they affect you?

Alternatives to Time Pattern of Organization

In contrast, some autobiographers, like some essayists, meander in their quest for the truth, so that the shape of their writing follows a nonlinear, nonchronological form. In the autobiography or memoir genre, these alternative forms generally play with themes or phases, linking them not in time order but additively or associatively. One idea leads to the next, which leads to the next. Some writers also compose in a fragmented fashion, writing many small essayistic pieces or many small vignettes. The order of these fragments is sometimes intuitive. Barrington speaks of a time she had a chronological narrative of tales in progress—the work that became her memoir *Lifesaving*—but did not feel she was getting anywhere with it. She then had a dream about some lifesaving classes she had taken as a child, and when she awakened, she wrote down her dream. Finally, acting intuitively, she inserted lines from the dream story between the stories in her narrative. The lines turned out to relate closely to the already written stories and worked to provide the themes and meanings the author was seeking. Thus, there are some conventions—things people usually do—but no hard and fast rules on ordering creative nonfiction.

▶ *Write Now! Exploring Story*

Taking phases you have identified from your timeline, write three or four different introductory paragraphs for your autobiography. Next, freewrite or sketch an imaginative, meandering path for your piece. Use associations and accident, fragments of vignettes, and sensory memories. Don't be afraid to try something different in autobiographical writing. Ideas may occur to you in the process of inventing or as you are finally editing the piece. Listen to your intuitions at whatever point they occur, even if it is after publication.

　　To understand yourself in an imaginative way, write a piece in your journal on this conundrum: Who am I when I am not me? Who we are *not* can be a very revealing topic. ◀

The Shape of Stories

Another triangle—that of rising action, climax, and denouement—enters the scene when we speak of stories. (See Figure 3.1.) This movement should be familiar from literature classes. But what is a story? Early in the twentieth century, critics such as E. M. Forster began to describe stories by distinguishing story from plot. "The king died, and then the queen died" is a story. With the addition of causality, we have a plot: "The king died, and then the queen died of grief." Now the two events do not just stand, one following the other, but they have a relation of causality.

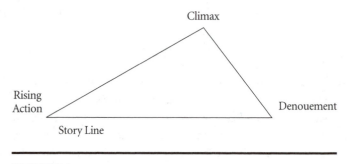

FIGURE 3.1

We absorb stories from our culture the way we absorb vitamin D from the sun. But when we begin to tell our own in writing, it is sometimes helpful to stop and look at just exactly what we do.

French theorist Roland Barthes described a story as a long sentence, with a grammar of its own. Following him, writing teacher Katharine Haake (Ostrom et al., 2000) asks, "What is the perfect grammar of the narrative?" And she also quotes Gertrude Stein: "Forget grammar and think about potatoes." Haake says the grammar of a story is "a sequence of events arranged according to a logic of placement, displacement, replacement, or equilibrium, disequilibrium, re-equilibrium"—again, our classic triangle. Stories may be more or less experimental, of course, with their authors trying to discover an appropriate structure. Nonetheless, when we read them, we often remake fragmented material into familiar "triangular" patterns in order to make sense of them.

In 1972 sociolinguist William Labov published an analysis of what he called "natural narratives"—oral stories told by his informants, adolescents from Harlem. After analyzing these stories, he divided them into not three, but six parts. Here are capsules of his parts in the order that the story was told:

1. Abstract (a preview or forecast of the meat of what is to come)
2. Orientation (context to help the reader understand time, place, characters)
3. Complicating action (the "disequilibrium" described earlier)
4. Evaluation (a moment when the teller reveals the center of gravity of the tale—what it means and why it is worth telling: "This was the most terrifying event of my life!")

5. Result or resolution (re-equilibrium)

6. Coda (returns the listener to the present time and closes off the story)

Written stories follow many of these moves, although some are easier to see than others. Is this a familiar pattern to you? Read some short memoirs, perhaps chapters in Annie Dillard's *An American Childhood*, and analyze them for these elements. We have learned "natural" or better, cultural patterns of telling stories from our families and cultural groups. Differences exist among groups, but we all hear and enjoy stories, so some common structures exist. It may be harder to reproduce stories in writing than to tell a tale with an audience present, but readers expect some of the same elements as when they are listeners.

Roles, Functions, and the Shape of Narratives

As we have mentioned, the structure of stories is passed down from generation to generation within a culture. Different groups assign different members to tell and safeguard their stories. Traditionally, African women told stories to children and other women in the kraals, the courtyard of their homes. With the disappearance of the physical structure of the village, women's storytelling roles declined. Yet this tradition may have helped prepare black South African women to pour out their stories at the end of apartheid when they were able to learn a rudimentary literacy (as my former Ph.D. student, Sandra Dickinson, tells me).

The shape of a story, what is valued, and how a story should be told is culture specific and changes over time. But some similarities have been found. For example, Vladimir Propp, the Russian literary theorist of the 1920s, analyzed the structure of fairy tales. He found many of them have structures and roles in common. Common "functions" in a tale were "constant and limited" (Scholes et al., 1995, 62), so that no matter how many tales Propp analyzed, he never counted more than 31 functions. These include such movements as "An interdiction is addressed to the hero," "The interdiction is violated," "One member of a family either lacks something or desires to have something," "The lack is made known and the hero is allowed to go or dispatched," "The hero leaves home," "The initial misfortune or lack is liquidated," and "The hero is married and ascends to the throne" (adapted from Scholes et al., 1995, 63–64). These functions can be grouped into a structure similar to the triangle discussed earlier, with the preparation, complication, and resolution.

Propp also found that fairy tales shared similar character roles, which he boiled down into seven (really eight, as one is embedded in number 4):

1. The villain
2. The donor or provider
3. The helper
4. The princess or sought-for person, and her father.
5. The dispatcher
6. The hero, seeker, or victim
7. The false hero

One character may fill several of these roles, which have been found to be common to much fiction. Another theorist described six roles:

1. Mars—opposition
2. Moon—helper
3. Sun—desired object
4. Balance (scales)—arbiter, rewarder
5. Earth—ultimate beneficiary
6. Lion—will, one who desires

These narrative roles or these positions for characters, abstracted from many, many Western stories, are found in some form in narratives. It would be surprising if you could read—or write—a story bearing no marks of these general character descriptions. Each of the last six, because they are suggestive and visual, might be used for journal writing exercises alone or in combination. You may want to discuss one of them with your writing group before free-writing on one or more for 10 minutes or more.

Common Roles and Scripts

We have learned that because stories bear a culture's experience and wisdom, they have common roles and model life scripts for characters as well as listeners. These are often at the base of our received cultural scripts, but they contain vestiges of a former culture's problems and solutions. These forms have much power, and while they also carry wisdom, they are seductive and bear critical analysis. For example, I once found that I had written not one but a series of pieces that, when scrutinized, took the form of the nursery tale "The Three Bears." One thing was always too big or great, while another was too small or lacking, and finally, one was just right. Once we begin and intuitively sense a familiar pattern, if we are not careful, the form takes over and seems to desire the pattern's completion. But we can ask ourselves: Is this honestly and strictly, factually my life experience? I have seen many young women trying to approximate the stories of *Cinderella* or, even more familiarly, *Beauty and the Beast*. Are these ancient tales our own? Can we change them, or must we just accept them today? Clarissa Pinkola Estes's *Women Who Run with the Wolves* explores both positive and negative myths for women and is replete with fascinating examples of life scripts.

Sidonie Smith's (1987) *A Poetics of Women's Autobiography* locates the origin of autobiography as a genre in the late Middle Ages and the Renaissance. Her premise is that these origins shaped spaces available to women in texts for centuries to come. Cultural conditions brought about by changing Christianity during that period left four primary roles or life scripts available to women in European literature: the nun, the queen, the wife, and the witch. During that time, women could gain authority if they embraced the religious functions of the virgin, performing roles valued by the Church, such as administrators, educators, and missionaries. However, these women could not become priests or pope and thus remained marginalized.

The political role of queen was another sanctioned function. Several women came to the throne during the Renaissance, providing the pattern for this script: Mary, Queen of Scots; Elizabeth I; and Catherine de Medici. "As the exceptional woman becomes a representative man, her female nature is repressed," Smith explained (35), which perpetuated patriarchal values.

Most women during that time were wives—the third cultural role represented in literature. They made valued cultural and economic contributions. With the Reformation, a new kind of wifehood emerged—the leisured, more middle-class style of wife. Marriage and childbirth were positive aspects of women's general negative roles. Honesty and chastity were therefore the key values associated with the role of wife.

The fourth role, that of witch, dispensed with honesty and chastity and was active rather than passive. The role of witch represents all repressed violence, both sexual and verbal. The powerful witch could make men impotent, but, in turn, powerful men could burn her at the stake. "Life scripts and autobiographical inscription of women become the mirror before which the story of man assumes its privileges. . . . " Smith writes (37). " 'Autobiography' then is ultimately an assertion of the arrival and embeddedness in the phallic order." Although we are here talking about the cultural roles for females, Smith also calls for an examination of how male roles are also shaped by necessarily fitting into a system that contains particular women's roles.

Gender roles embedded in our culture's literary traditions may allow or constrain our autobiographies. Myths of various types and stereotypes, especially ethnic ones, can be internalized and reproduced unthinkingly. Writers in formerly colonized countries have written eloquently about this problem in their autobiographies. Ken Bugul, a Senegalese woman, writes of herself as an African female in white Europe in *The Abandoned Baobab*. Gandhi's autobiography, *The Story of My Experiments with Truth*, bears witness to social upheaval, torture, and imprisonment, as do a number of other autobiographies by postcolonial subjects. Franz Fanon has written about the need for formerly colonized people to reject their colonial subject positions in order to tell the truth.

In this complex world in which we live and have our being, we take many subject positions and play many roles, roles that participate in common ideologies and myths. In a specific setting, such as a classroom, one self is elicited or hooked (the "student")—or "hailed," to use Louis Althusser's term. In another setting, perhaps in a medical clinic, the persona of the suffering patient comes out, whether your patient persona is stoic or whiny (or perhaps in this setting you are the consummately professional doctor or her assistant). In speaking to our mothers, we present one face and voice, and in speaking to a dog or a child, we usually use quite another. Because we perform so many roles and contain so many real and potential personae, we are truly multiple socially.

More than one thinker has suggested that our true freedom as an individual may lie either in the unscripted gaps between these social roles or in the tactical way we choose to combine and deploy our roles in our everyday lives. But who are we *really* outside our already-shaped and shaping roles and scripts? This remains another secret of life, the mystery of the phenomenon we call the self—one we must explore but need not answer in writing autobiography.

Exploring Roles and Selves

Composition, like writers, must proceed on faith, in the full belief that the writing subject controls this [writing] production. But it must also renounce that faith, . . . in order to explain the act of writing more accurately.

—*Raul Sanchez, 2001*

The foregoing quotation tries to chart a middle path between our being shaped solely by our own individual will and powers and our being determined by outside cultural and material forces. The following example and writing activities will let you explore this interesting middle space for yourself.

Asian Americans, many of whom have been in this country for three or more generations, have resisted "disappearing like raindrops" into the sea of white Americans. This resistance to forgetting a complex history of struggles with the dominant culture can be seen in their writing, which often works to "claim America for Asian Americans," one literary critic writes. In fact, much writing by Asian Americans focuses on claiming an American identity. What is the cause of this? Is it a simple wish to blend in, a tired giving in to years of oppression, or is it a search for an identity built on a foundation of past cultural identity?

Stereotyping is also a problem, for both men and women. Asian American women are often viewed in the role of exotic sex objects, passively trying to please men. And men are often depicted in roles we see on TV or in film, as evil warlords or obsequious servants, Fu Manchus or Charlie Chans.

Cultural critic Kim (1987) reports that in the "Dear Abby" advice column a few years past, two Irish Americans expressed impatience with "Orientals'" discomfort at being asked "What are you?" when they are first introduced to Caucasians. Abby printed a typical Asian-American response:

What am I? Why, I'm a person like everyone else. . . . "Where did you come from?" would be an innocent question when one Caucasian asks it of another, but when it is asked of an Asian, it takes on a different tone. . . . When I say, "I'm from Portland, Oregon!" they are invariably surprised . . . because they find it hard to believe that an Asian-looking person is actually . . . American. . . . Being white is not a prerequisite for being . . . American . . . and it is high time everyone realized it." ("Dear Abby" excerpt, quoted in Kim, 1987).

▶ *Write Now! Who Am I?*

- No matter what your ethnic background, imagine that you have been asked what you are in a situation that made it clear you were being wrongly identified. Write a brief letter to "Dear Abby" to set it straight. Begin like the foregoing letter: "What am I?" Then go on to sort out for your readers how you wish to be identified and addressed.

- List as many social roles as you can, roles you play in your everyday life. For example, each day I am a partner, a daughter, a teacher, a consumer, a colleague, and a friend. Try for about 20; sociologists have found that we each play many more. After you list your roles, write a short description of who you are in each role. What kinds of passions and concerns are involved? What key words or topics emerge that you might like to write about? Do a 10-minute journal session over as many as you deem worthy.

- Choose a piece of autobiographical writing you have done in the past. Who are you as the narrator in telling that story? Which of your roles are expressed?

- Imagine: How might we be different in a different setting and society where we had different roles to play? ◀

Roles and Voice

The role of the narrator in your autobiography has much to do with that mysterious writing phenomenon called "voice." Barrington (1997, 21) believes that voice is all-important in memoir, which "requires that the reader feel *spoken to.*" This means that your autobiographical writing should be close to the way you (in one of your primary roles) speak. This is not an easy task to assign yourself. Whether you speak in a rural or an urban dialect, with working-class patterns, a black vernacular, or Spanglish, trying to write as you speak can sometimes make you look more like a cartoon than a writer. That is because conventions for representing dialect have not yet been worked out and agreed upon by readers. Be aware that many other writers in English have had and are having this difficulty today, not only in the United States but around the world. Sometimes, writing mostly in standard written English, with just a few cues to your speech community, works well to give the sound of your speech. Take a look at Geoffrey Nunberg's (2001) *The Way We Talk Now* if you are interested in a linguist's view of language and the cultural implications of changes in language.

Autobiography as a form is a hybrid of fictional and essayist tactics. Memoirist Barrington (1997, 22) writes that "the author's voice, musing on a true story, is all important." Voice also comes into play with the credibility of a narrative, for the faith that the story is a true narrative has "*an effect on the reader*—he reads it believing it to be a true story, which in turn requires the writer to be an unflinchingly reliable narrator" to keep this contract with the reader (26). This may serve as the basis for autobiographical voice, and yet voices are myriad in this genre of life narrative. For example, here is a memoir by cyberwriter Kathy Acker. Analyze the narrator's role in this piece and comment on related qualities of voice. Then write a memoir that explores your own history of learning to write and to find your voice.

Kathy Acker

"Dead Doll Humility"

. . . ONE NIGHT CAPITOL GAVE THE FOLLOWING SCENARIO TO HER WRITER DOLL:

As a child in sixth grade in a North American school, won first prize in a poetry contest. In late teens and early twenties, entered New York City poetry world. Prominent Black Mountain poets, mainly male, taught or attempted to teach her that a writer becomes a writer when and only when he finds his own voice. . . .

* * *

Since wanted to be a writer, tried hard to find her own voice. Couldn't. But still loved to write. Loved to play with language. Language was material like clay or paint. Loved to play with verbal material, build up slums and mansions, demolish banks and half-rotten buildings, even buildings which she herself had constructed, into never-before-seen, even unseeable jewels.

To her, every word wasn't only material in itself, but also sent out like beacons, other words. _Blue_sent out _heaven_ and _The Virgin_. Material is rich.

I didn't create language, writer thought. Later she would think about ownership and copyright. I'm constantly being given language. Since this language-world is rich and always changing, flowing, when I write, I enter a world which has complex relations and is, perhaps, illimitable. This world both represents and is human history, public memories and private memories turned public, the records and actualizations of human intentions. . . . So where is 'my voice'?

Wanted to be a writer.

Since couldn't find 'her voice', decided she'd first have to learn what a Black Mountain poet meant by 'his voice'. What did he do when he wrote?

A writer who had found his own voice presented a view-point. Created a meaning. The writer took a certain amount of language, verbal material, forced that language to stop radiating in multiple, even unnumerable directions, to radiate in only one direction so there could be his meaning.

The writer's voice wasn't exactly this meaning.

The writer's voice was a process, how he had forced the language to obey him, his will. The writer's voice is the voice of the writer-as-God.

Writer thought, Don't want to be God; have never wanted to be God. . . .

Want to play. Be left alone to play. Want to be a sailor who journeys at every edge and even into the unknown. See strange sights, see. . . .

    * * *

4

Autobiography, Media, and Technology: Old and New

After a long period of the dominance of the book as the central medium of communication, the screen has now taken that place. This is leading to more than a mere displacement of writing. It is leading to an inversion in semiotic power. The book and the page were the sites of writing. The screen is the site of the image—it is the contemporary canvas. The book and the page were ordered by the logic of writing; the screen is ordered by the logic of image.

—Gunther Kress, 2003

Different media provide different kinds of canvasses on which the writer of life narrative can work. Marshall McLuhan captured the attention of a generation with his dictum "The medium is the message," which was the famous title of his book first published in 1967. This was decades before the advent of the World Wide Web and proliferation of "new media." Although McLuhan's axiom may be a bit exaggerated, writers are learning more each day about just how much the medium affects us, framing and massaging not only our experience but our genres. In memoir and autobiography, new media have the potential to create new genres through changing opportunities for sharing and presentation of work.

New media include digitized text, which can be hyperlinked in combination with digital graphics, encompassing photography, video, and audio—all of which can be melded together on websites or in ebooks. New media exist today alongside traditional media, such as nondigital, noncomputerized journals and diaries, photographs, sound recordings, drawings and sketches, and video in the arsenal of autobiographers. As we use more and more digital possibilities, we become more like producers of our life narratives than writers. Whether you believe this is a good thing or not will determine how you proceed with your life narrative work. Many people still feel alienated from or even fearful of digital media, while they generally have come to accept and even love photography and other traditional media. Nevertheless, I believe we should not neglect to use media—old or new or both—in trying to share and understand our lives. Digital media have some distinct advantages in presentation and outreach and are getting easier and more widespread all the time.

The late technology critic Neil Postman (2003), author of many books on the media—including the now-canonical television critique *Amusing Ourselves to Death*—distinguishes pointedly between a technology and a medium. "As I see it, a technology is to a medium as the brain is to a mind," he writes (184). A technology or way of doing things only becomes a medium to Postman "as it insinuates itself into economic and political contexts. A technology, in other words, is merely a machine, a piece of hard-wiring," while "a medium is a social creation." This distinction allows him to understand—about e-learning, for example—how different social groups might use different technologies differently, and, significantly, that how a technology is used is usually not the only way it might be used. Technology offers a limited but open number of possible uses, while social conventions set mainstream uses.

Those who would never in the past have called themselves "autobiographers," or even writers, are even now turning the technology of the Internet into a medium for writing life narratives. But conventions of use are not yet set and are still fluid. Older technologies of text production, graphics, and publishing have already become media for autobiography, although some have been disappearing of late. (I still have a few mimeographed memoirs and Christmas letters around, but not many.) Postman advises us that technologies are not neutral but have a "predisposition" to be used in certain ways and not others. This means that we should explore the biases of any technology used in the service of autobiography and see what it might offer and delimit before we accept it wholeheartedly. Technologies and available media have changed throughout history, changing the possibilities and shapes of life narrative writing.

Consider this chapter's opening quote from Kress in a small group discussion. What do you think the "logic of image" is, in contrast to the "logic of writing"?

Websites as New Sites for Life Narratives: The Hypertextual Life

Personal web pages present a new technology for life narratives that is in the process of becoming an autobiographical medium, massaging the ways we present our stories and how readers react to them. These new opportunities for enhanced presentation act on our writing to transform the various genres of self-life writing, such as journals, diaries, and memoirs. Writing for and on the web transforms writing first by providing new possibilities for display and design. These apparent supplements to old forms are not really just slight additions, however; they revolutionize our writing itself.

Whereas, in the past, authors could supply photographs or drawings to publishers of their memoirs, these were limited by the cost of production. Memoirs themselves were limited by publishing costs. Today, aspiring authors who can beg, borrow, or steal computer equipment and Internet connections can be their own publishers. They can obtain space to put up a website and "publish" to their sites. Many personal websites have become, in essence, acts of autobiographical writing. In 1994, for example, a student in my undergraduate advanced composition class set up a free website, using Geocities.com space, as part of a class assignment in autobiographical writing. Today, he has his own site, www.Bacchusland.com, where he tells visitors about his personal life, life trajectory, and academic interests. (See Figure. 4.1.)

So how does writing for the web change autobiography? This medium is so new that forms are still evolving. It is still possible to present text that looks like a typed paper manuscript, although it is only

FIGURE 4.1

a visual facsimile. (As my colleague Laura Gibbs notes, it is amusing that the term *manuscript* has stayed with us long after the invention of type!) More and more, however, such pages look out of place. Long texts on the web can now be sectioned off, subheaded, and linked with "internal links" to make reading easier. Web readers are getting used to even more sophisticated and attractive designs for displaying their own texts or "external links" to others' pages.

Writing for the Web

Your text will be more conformable to the web format if you conceive or write it as hypertext from the start. This means breaking it up into shorter segments with clear focuses, preferably signaled by headings of the appropriate size (in hypertext markup language—HTML—and, in most word processing programs, Headings 1, 2, and 3, in descending order of size and logic). This chapter will not attempt to explain the technical aspect of producing web pages but will restrict itself to how websites are and might be used to publish life narratives and associated materials.

If you have been working on life narrative assignments and have some text in word processing format, you can display those files on a personal website. In fact, a website makes a perfect medium in which to present a linked portfolio of life narrative pieces. But to conceive a personal website for life narratives means first doing some paper and pencil planning, sometimes called storyboarding or designing web architecture. Heidi Schultz (2000), in *The Elements of Electronic Communication*, advises using colored index cards to represent "folders" for your website. You can lay these out on a table, or you can simply draw and redraw plans for your site on a scrap of paper or sketchpad. Schultz advises planning no more than three levels: home page, main links, and sublink levels and writing on each card your text and the links you plan (see Schultz, 2000, 90–108).

Architecture is a good term to use for this process of planning your autobiographical website: Like the design of a building, your design will control the flow of visitors to your site. Using this analogy, readers enter an entry hall, which opens onto a great room, with all rooms off that linking in a circular or network flow. Or you might have a "shotgun" house, which makes it necessary to go through one room to get to the next in a linear pattern. The main entry room controlling the flow is your index or home page. Your entry page can be a well-designed hall to introduce your house, or readers can enter the great room and see hallways leading to all your work immediately. The more linear you make your flow, the more mouse clicks readers have to make to get to your work. The more networked you make your site, the fewer clicks that are necessary. It is worth planning the architecture of your site before proceeding, as it saves time implementing the site in the long run.

Plans Up Front: Design

After you plan the site architecture, you will have the fun of designing the look that will represent you. This is not unlike the interior design of a home, for the pages create a structure of feeling and an ethos, giving your site credibility and a style and tone—formal or informal, serious, ironic, funny, or just plain silly. Many programs and websites are available to help you with web design, such as the popular program Dreamweaver and online help with that program.

I have searched for interior design websites, such as Martha Stewart's site or paint company sites, to browse for color schemes, but many preset, preprogrammed selections are available. You will need to choose appropriate colors for the background, which can be plain or patterned "wallpaper," and colors for the type. The most important thing here is to provide enough contrast between print and background to make the site readable, as autobiography webmasters necessarily take their textual components seriously.

In order to unify your portfolio site, create a template for each page that allows for a consistent look from page to page. Web page programs all allow for such a template function, although lately the style sheet (CSS) has become more important in determining how a page should look. Many websites today contain "frames"—separate, often boxed windows within a main window—but these are a major impediment to web accessibility. As web guru Nielsen puts it: "Frames: Just Say No" (http://www.useit.com/alertbox/9612.html). Style sheets and templates help you easily create new pages that have a "family resemblance" to your others and carry the necessary navigational buttons. You will still be able to make changes to the basic template design on any particular page when you need to.

Since graphics are possible and desirable in this medium, the "family crest" assignment is a good place to start to think about a personal graphic logo or catchphrase. Also, it is now fairly easy to scan old family photographs and mementos for your hyperlinked autobiographical pages. My eldest brother performed an invaluable family service by scanning all of our parents' old photographs he had taken box by box from mother and distributing to each of us five children a set of CDs that contained them all. I created for myself a digitized slide show of myself growing up (using a free slide show program I downloaded). It would be possible to link such a slide show to a website. However, the number one problem I have seen with personal websites is excessive load time, caused by improper handling or overuse of graphic and audio files. You may find your pictures charmingly irresistible and the load time tolerable, but few visitors will want to wait while your site loads pictures of you that are too big for one page. But do use graphics and photographs wisely to liven up your site. Of course, the availability of high-speed connections and increased bandwidth have made loading much faster, but good design takes readership into account. It is still good citizenship to design for speed.

The watchwords of web design are simplicity, contrast, a unified look, clear signals of where you have been and where you might go with links, adequate white space, and eye-relieving graphics. These make autobiographical websites more usable and readable. Guidelines similar to readability studies from print media are not out of place here. They are frequently violated in this medium, however, where hierarchies of authority are challenged and even readability cannot be defended as an absolute standard. Yet I wonder why it is that in a new medium, where there is already a "blooming, buzzing confusion," designers choose styles that only enhance the chaos? I'm afraid that as a middle-aged Baby Boomer I find it hard to understand and accept that there is a new aesthetic, appealing to younger users who find it pleasing to have what is to me an overstimulating visual effect. Older, cleaner designs may be more usable to most people, but I am aware that they look stodgy to younger eyes. Suit yourself, but be aware that there are limitations to human focus and attention, even if they are in transformation or if we do not quite know what they are. A clean, Zen style will always provide a place of quiet relief on the noisy web, but I recognize that this may not be your style.

Ask yourself the following questions:

- Will your homepage have a simple graphic and entry links or will it begin your life narrative and provide links for wider access? The homepage has been compared to a book cover. Does your homepage contain the same orienting conventions of a book cover or a title page?

- How many clicks will it take to get to the "bottom" layer of your site? (No more than three is recommended, but there are no firm rules.)

- Is the look of your website something you are happy to present as iconic or representative of your personality, your style?

- Have you broken up the text and provided clear signals for readers in terms of subheadings and links?

- Do you have adequate graphic elements to relieve text-heavy pages? Do you have few enough to keep down the load time for your page?

- Is the type large enough and does it contrast with the background enough to make your text readable?

- Have you provided appropriate links within your text to expanded or related information or graphics?

Blogging Your Life: Weblogs as Public Journals

Newspapers are filled with headlines about the newest website craze—weblogging, or blogging. This essentially means writing and posting a daily or periodic journal or diary on the web. Often, readers are invited to respond with their own postings, or at the least, they can correspond with the blogger via a "mail-to" address on the website. (As my blog-savvy colleague Laura Gibbs points out, vocabulary, as in the word "post," more than actual technology, distinguishes "the world of blogs and the world of web pages.") As with any new media, the news media trumpets weblogging problems in sensational headlines such as "Dating a Blogger, Read All About It" and "Blogging Gone Awry," both in the

Sunday *New York Times* "Styles" section of May 18, 2003. There are some new problems with this new genre, but the same old problems faced by traditional memoirists also still exist. These include "hurt feelings, newly wary friends and relatives, and the occasional inflamed employer," according to one informant.

As expert David Weinberger wisely advises: "All writing is a form of negotiation between the reader and writer over what constitutes responsibility. Because blogs are a new form, the negotiation can easily go awry" (St. John). He goes on to explain that the confessional nature of blogs has "redrawn the line between what's private and public." One blogger was critical of her parents, who were Mormons. When they found out, as many who are "blogged" often do, "all hell broke loose," the blogger said (11). "If you're publishing under your own name, they'll find out," she said. "I was extremely naive." Friends of bloggers have become wary, and there is a new public neurosis—fear of being blogged. If everyone is a potential journalist and life is only grist for the blogging mill, conversation can be dangerous. Thus, the genre of conversation can be affected: Everyday chitchat becomes fair game, so rules must be established as to what is on and off the record.

That being the case, why would bloggers publish personal confessions and daily minutia in a public forum? Experts say some bloggers want a readership, like any journalist or author, and they are trying to build one through juicy entries. Others say these bloggers are just attention seekers. Yet while there is a long tradition of privacy in journaling, there is also a centuries-old tradition of shared or public journaling. Families have long kept journals for family records, and Victorian parents—usually mothers—and children kept diaries together as a means of communication and close sharing. Many journals were kept privately but meant to be published one day, so the line between public and private has always been wavy. Nonetheless, these new opportunities for public journaling and interaction are providing a new medium and new genres. Some blogs are more private and voyeuristic, while others are mixed private and public and some are entirely informational and public-spirited. There are now group blogs, and some are even closed-group blogs, like a family or community journal or a blog for a writing class—see http://www.culturecat.net/index.php. Group blogs have recently been enabled by new services at Blogger.com.

A blog can be a way to represent yourself in a new medium or to fashion and display a new subjectivity. For example, Susan Smith Nash uses web pages and blogs in her beyondutopia.com site to represent herself virtually in her varied aspects as a creative intellectual. As blogs change all the time, it is best to go to a search engine, such as Google.com, and look for yourself—but here are a few that were popular or interesting at the time I was researching blogs myself:

Examples: Blogs containing life writing from those nominated for "bloggies" (www.fairvue.com/bloggies/2004) or other notable sites. [Last accessed 6/8/2004.]

- http://www.rebeccablood.net/handbook/excerpts/weblog_ethics.html
  Award-winning blog by Rebecca Blood, Rebecca's Pocket, contains a section on weblog ethics.

- http://www.simplebits.com
  This site won the best-designed weblog in the 2004 bloggies. SimpleBits is the "hypertext home" of web design consultant and author, Dan Cederholm.

- http://tequilamockingbird.blogspot.com/
  This best-kept-secret bloggie winner is a good site to consider personal issues and public/private dilemmas of blogs.

- http://www.margaretcho.com/blog/
  Comedian Margaret Cho's blog won a bloggie for being the most humorous, although the latest material may not aim to tickle your funny bone.

- http://www.boingboing.net/
  Author Russ Kick's winning weblog Boing Boing, passes on links to favorite spots on the web as well as posting autobiographical news.

- http://accordionguy.blogware.com/
  Joey DeVila's autobiographical and pictorial The Adventures of Accordion Guy in the Twenty-First Century, runner-up in the weblog of the year 2004 overall blog category.

- http://www.sinosplice.com/~laowaimono/
  The Laowai Monologues, by Hank Jones, a detailed account of the struggles and difficulties of an American teacher living and teaching in the small city of Huaibei, Anhui Province, China.

- http://adverbatim.auliya.net/Adverbatim
  An award-winning writer's aesthetically pleasing site to display her poetry and reflections.

- http://www.fairytale-ending.com/
  A sixties-themed Fairy Tale Endings weblog—formerly Ordinary Miracles—is still about the life and times of Niki, a Toronto university student.

- http://www.hchamp.com/
  Heather Champ's weblog links to the photoblog site, itself contains wonderful photography, and is also a Lifetime Achievement Award from the Bloggies, as she has published since October 1, 2000.

Blogging: How to Start

It is possible to keep a weblog on a web page after you have established your site just by posting text, by which I mean typing in a message. Sometimes a blogger invites readers by joining a network of bloggers, then asking for comments and feedback. There are individual, closed group blogs and open-to-all community blogs. Your blog could include features to interest a reader, such as favorite websites or even your own cartoon (JonathanVanGieson.com). A weblog can actually be your own newsletter—published by, for, and about you. There is such variation in blogs from service to service that it is difficult to make generalizations. The difference between paid and free services is enormous. (Defining blogs and distinguishing them from many other features of websites is hard to do even when you get into the technical side of things.)

To create a blog, you will need a blog browser, which can be downloaded for free from many sites. Blogger.com was one of the first and offers many individual and group free services, but competitors have sprung up as the market has heated up; for example, see http://blogRolling.com or http://www.movabletype.org/, for more specialized services. These programs allow instant publishing to your website. They make it easy for you to add links or other material and for your readers to respond. This chapter will not explain the technology, as that information can easily be found on these sites or by searching for other web publishing sites for blogging.

Why, What, and How to Blog, in Brief

The website JonathanVanGieson.com answers the question of why to blog satirically, saying, in part:

> This Weblog—or "Blog" in common parlance—will stand for the ages. Each inspirational moment of my famous life, each clandestine meeting with my famous friends, each night of debauchery, each drug-induced alcoholic stupor, each embarrassing arrest, will be accurately reported here. It is my fond hope that the young will be able to turn to this text as a guidebook to life. Or, at very least, a manual.

Writers and others, such as consultants who must network or need to be known, are frequent bloggers. The popularity of blogging is recent, however; in its beginnings, it was a more marginal activity, attracting many quirky and outside-the-mainstream participants.

Blogs have subgenres, from impersonal newsletter to personal newsletter to diary and journal, to day-in-the life confessionals (see Caterina.net). Postings can include chronological commentary, movies, reviews, drawings, photographs, music, favorite links, and anything else you can imagine. Check out examples on the web to use as models or anti-models. Most blogs—even the impersonal newsletter blogs—contain some form of life narrative. What makes them life writing is the chronological format, in which the accretion of facts unknown to the author as well as the readers acquires, over time, a dramatic, insightful aura of reality.

Finally, I would recommend that everyone who has a website (especially an interactive blog) set up "terms of service" or "terms of use"—agreements by which, in linking to your site, readers agree to your particular terms of use (which might even forbid you to sue them!). You may want to examine some terms of use statements on the web, and Chapter 5 provides some general advice for those writing life narratives that would hold here as well. Common sense and the general ethic of treating others as you would want to be treated go a long way here. Consider friendly terms of use statements such as the following editorial policy for interactive blogs:

> I reserve the right to delete comments. Please keep it civil. I am generally pro-free speech, but I know troll or a flame when I see one. Some speech makes a civilized discussion impossible and drives

more polite speakers away. I have no tolerance for spam: I get to decide what constitutes spam on my site.

http://www.zenhaiku.com/archives/clay_shirky_on_web_logs_and_publishing.html (July 30, 2003, 1:30 P.M.)

Obviously, such policies are necessary only for interactive websites; if you have a personal website that carries only your own postings, you would be the only one writing in that space, so you wouldn't need such a policy.

▶ *Reflect Now! Public and Private: Life Narratives Online*

- What experiences have you had with new media such as websites and autobiographical blogs? How have they changed your thinking about what is private and what is public? What advantages and disadvantages do you see in presenting autobiographical narratives in these forms?

- Review blogs that end up nominated for "bloggies" at http://www.fairvue.com/?feature=awards2004. What criteria are used to judge these blogs?

- The size of the web makes it easy to keep a blog without your name on it and without an email link. Does that make it "public" or "private"? ◀

Oral Life Narratives on TV Talk Shows

Oral life narrative is a staple of daytime TV talk shows such as those of Oprah, Dr. Phil, Sally Jesse Raphael, and many others. In just two shows recently, Oprah listened to the stories of betrayed women whose husbands had cheated on them, heard from some of the men themselves, presented a Wall Street executive who had lost his $20 million through smoking crack cocaine, and elicited the story of AJ of the Back Street Boys, who is a recovering addict. Dr. Phil counseled couples in sexless marriages the same day. Oprah explained on the air that the reason she has people tell their private stories on air is that other people might see themselves and share a "kernel of hope."

Autobiography scholar Janice Peck (1996) critiques these TV shows in which hosts and guests produce narrated lives and viewers consume life stories. What is invisible is the institutional framework in which the personal stories are told, she argues. Often, "They address social conflicts that can never be fully resolved on TV while holding out the possibility that talking will lead to, or is itself a form of resolution" (134).

She says the issues are always framed, as in "Couples who fight about money!" not "Money, Power, and Gender." No wandering off the narrow focus is allowed. This takes the problem out of the social framework and makes it solely a personal problem, presented for entertainment, under the TV personality system, where there is a lack of equality and reciprocity between host and guest, justifying considering the forced confessions "therapy."

▶ *Reflect Now! Life Narratives on Television*

- Do you or members of your class watch TV talk shows? How is your notion of reality affected by these shows? How are people's life stories elicited and framed?

- Discuss one show in particular and discuss whether the revelations of personal lives contribute to the public good or are a bad influence on viewers.

- How have notions of public and private changed as a result of these shows. Watch oral life narratives presented on television for one week and evaluate them in light of Peck's critique. ◀

New and Old Media: Revisiting Elements of Traditional Autobiography

Autobiographers have always gathered, meditated on, handled, or experienced nontextual objects and events in the world and their representations in various media in preparing their life narratives. Our words are always interlaced with other people's words and the things of the world when we weave our autobiographical discourses. Some of the specific things I am talking about here are genres in language: the recipe or the oral family tale; the landscape or event that the writer tries to capture with words; the object, such as your grandmother's wedding ring; or various media, including photographs, slides, paintings, home movies, audiotaped interviews or vignettes, or compilations—scrapbooks and memory books or baby books that incorporate photos and objects. All of these and other objects and media around you are grist for the autobiographical mill. (Incidentally, all can now be photographed and digitized to be used on a CD, in an ebook, or on an internet autobiography, but I leave it to you to investigate possibilities.)

▶ *Write Now! Nontextual Media*

Here are some suggestions for broadening your autobiographical discourse with nontextual media or using nontextual media to invent more autobiographical writing:

- *Drawings:* Peter R. Stillman (1989, 2), author of *Families Writing*, did sketches as gifts for his children as they were growing up. He would make a drawing on a phase of life and caption it, "When I was your age," adding a sentence or two about what it was like to be that age. ("When I was your age, I smoked my first cigarette. It was a Camel. I stole it from my mother, sat on my favorite rock, and lit up. I loved every minute of it." The sketch was of a boy on a rock, coughing.) Make a simple sketch of an event or phase of your life like Stillman's. Some of the following ideas were inspired by Stillman's book.

- *Sounds:* Capture the language of others by audiotaping or writing down creative, funny uses of language. Try to translate nonverbal sounds into text. Interview family members about family sagas, or get the family together and set up a tape recorder. You should always transcribe tapes so that they are usable for autobiographies.

- *Sight:* Translate a landscape or visual scene into "field notes," using both text and drawings. Note that you can use a long shot or a close-up and describe your field of vision from the foreground to the background, from left to right, or in a circular or spiral pattern.

- *Other senses:* Capture specific odors and translate them into writing. Smell is a sense very close to the emotions. Having sensory "odors" in your work can inject emotional tone without telling readers how to feel. The same can be done with touch and other senses, such as physical orientation, balance, and movement.

- Collect old letters sent to you or sent to or written by your family members.

- Make a book of recipes, and write stories about memories of eating each food.

- Write about objects belonging to you or your family. My own mother keeps family treasures in an old cedar chest—objects my father brought back after serving in the occupying army in Japan after World War II, handkerchiefs given to her by girlfriends at a handkerchief shower when she married, an old doll belonging to her sister, a Kiowa beaded purse. I could write for days on the objects in this chest and my feelings about them over time.

- Make a scrapbook or keepsake book of paper or flat objects or write about a family keepsake book. My older brother has digitized my maternal grandmother's high school memory book from the 1920s. What a gift!

- Get the family together, get out old photographs or paintings, and have family members explain who is in the photos and the circumstances under which they came to be. Tape or take notes of the proceedings. Also, take a photograph and meditate on it, then write in your journal.

- Make a list of the important automobiles you remember. What was the first car you remember riding in or your parents owning? What was the first car you owned? Make a list of each car's memories for journaling or essay writing.

- On a sheet of paper, draw the floorplan of the first house you remember living in. Label each room and brainstorm a list of memories for each room. Write about a phase of life in the house or about feelings and sensations about the house.

Here is an example of journaling I did after viewing a picture of myself as a four-year-old in front of my grandmother's house.

Catherine Hobbs
"House of Dreams"

FIGURE 4.2   Writing, from picture of author and brother Steve in Grandfather's boat in front of "Grandmother Ray's house"

The old house that was there from long before my birth until I was in high school has been gone 35 years now. Mother lived there from her older school days until she married my father in 1948 after graduating from high school and becoming a bookkeeper at the gas company. She lived with her mother, my Grandmother Mildred Ray, her father Leon, and her younger sister Margaret, the name she still calls my younger sister Jeannie. Jeannie and her older brother Hank both visited the house, but my youngest sister Susan was born too late.

The house, two stories, with a large attic and a curved, wrap-around and columned porch, was perhaps at one time a farm house, although it was just off the main Market Street of town. I can see now that it must have once had an outhouse, as the bathroom was tacked on to the kitchen at the rear, to one side of a now-enclosed porch. The floor always leaned a bit in the bathroom, once you got outside the large, sunny kitchen to the porch or mud room leading to the bathroom. Perhaps however, the house was designed for a town dweller destined to take in boarders. A family headed by a man named Donald lived upstairs, which was an apartment. The front hallway was held in common by all inhabitants and the frosted glass-paned door locked with a common old skeleton key. Just the sound of that word made me think the house was haunted, along with the creepiness of the empty but furnished rooms upstairs once Donald et al moved out. The attic, forbidden to us but which we sneaked into on most visits, was truly of the past, with marvelous dusty mysteries, including my great-grandmother's old spinning wheel.

I see now that the front bedroom off the central hallway to the right upon entering the long hallway into the house might have also been designed for a boarder. It only connected to the rest of the first floor by a secret door into the closet of the adjacent bedroom. The boarder in that large, high-ceilinged room would then have had a separate room and been able to come and go through the front hallway without disturbing the rest of the household.

My grandmother's living room and suite of rooms then (my grandfather having mostly "gone fishing" for most of my childhood), consisted of a large living room, whose door opened on the left of the entry hall. The living room, lighted by bare hanging lightbulbs turned on by black on-and-off buttons in a lightplate, was furnished, I see now, in a fifties modernist style, with sleek plastic and aluminum furniture that seems now to me like that of old train station waiting rooms. In that room, my brother Steve and I watched the first television of our lives, on a small, round-screened RCA. The signal came from a 50-foot or so aluminum tower just outside in the front yard, a tower my brother and I were forbidden to climb although I recall doing so on more than one occasion. My brother and I watched Captain Kangaroo, Zorro, Superman, and Lawrence Welk, a regular show of my grandmother's that my brother still watches but that has always been a joke to me.

Past the living room was a hallway with a small telephone stand and then a dark bedroom that smelled strongly of sweat and powder that offended my nose when I was small. My grandmother owned a small cafe a few blocks from the old house, where she cooked and served car hop fried foods, lunches, and beer. Perhaps the smell that inhabited her bedroom and bathroom emanated from the fryer, her powder, or her house, but it helped to drive me out of doors or across the street to my paternal grandparents' house catty corner across the street. Whereas Grandmother Ray always had hard candies, my father's mother had cinnamon rolls and fresh fried donuts to tempt us.

But when it came time to sleep, we returned to the creepy house to sleep in a bedroom reached by passing through Grandmother's room. This room, a junk room, had old army cots with heavy scratchy wool blankets. My older brother who was almost a twin to me growing up remembers the turtledoves cooing in the long mornings when we were told to lie in bed and not disturb the adults who had stayed up way too late the night before. My own memories are those of a child with a nervous nature. The water-stained ceiling in the room allowed me to project all sorts of ghouls from my imagination. The insecure opening at the back of the closet into the third bedroom also worried me, as I feared the front door would be left open and a stranger would sneak in to molest us through the secret closet door. One night, I was awakened (or not) by a menacing shape on the heavy pull-down shade, a silhouette before the street lamp shining behind the window. I called out, and mother came to my side, although she told me it had been a nightmare, attributing it to a scary television program seen that day. I don't know whether to believe her or not to this day.

As the house was on a corner, the yard was spacious, and in addition, included an empty lot on one side. My older brother holds fond memories of a metal storage shed in that yard where Grandpa Ray's illegal games of chance (pinball machines!) and his Navy memorabilia were stored. Once in the shed, he found and expropriated a military wrist compass from WWII he wore for years. I loved the way the dial turned in the dime-sized bubble of air in the center of the round face where the arrow spun around. My brother was sad years later when the plastic aged, cracked, and all the water ran out.

Despite my stinginess with time and affection, my Grandmother Ray loved me, her first girl grandchild. Had she not dressed me in early grade school, I might have gone to school quite naked, or at least more ragged than I was already. I often dream of her house, which was burned down in a firefighter training session years ago after mother inherited it and could not sell it, could no longer pay the insurance for the uninhabitable habitation. Today a non-descript brick ranch house occupies the site without filling it with its presence. No tabby cats steal out from under the broad porch steps and no profusion of zinnias welcomes the passerby. There are no longer any blind upper windows to send a thrill or chill up the spine. All children deserve a dwelling like this for their dreams, but not all are so lucky. ◄

Autobiographical Essays and Radio: A Funny Combination

I hear more about recently published life narratives—as well as hearing actual life narratives themselves—on National Public Radio than in any other forum outside autobiography journals, or perhaps the *New York Times Book Review*. Many who write short, pithy autobiographical essays in this genre submit them and ultimately read them on public radio. Most of the essays, for whatever reason, are light and humorous, if not downright funny. I recently heard a show discussing and sharing the autobiography of a young woman who had recently died of cystic fibrosis. She was able to reach me because she had gained insight—not just into her own mortal illness, but into the human condition—and offered it to listeners gently, with a light touch. Let's look for a moment at writing for this intimate sound medium and what might make something funny on it.

Nancy Davidoff Kelton (1997, 173) author and teacher of autobiography, refers to Charlie Chaplin as saying, "Life is a tragedy from the close shot and a comedy from the long shot." The point here is that to take in hard truths, we need distance. Readers identify with those who struggle, and we all can relate to those who flounder through life. The most serious and traumatic events have been sensitively portrayed in this medium humorously. This should teach us something about the rest of our life narrative writing.

Kelton writes, "I think the Number One Thing that makes people laugh is The Truth. The Truth with a curlycue at the end. It's a special way of looking at life. One that requires distance. Perspective. A sense of the ridiculous." What is funny? The unexpected. Surprising turns. Off-the-wall situations. The absurd. If something strikes you, write it down. If something makes you laugh, write it down. Think of the comedians you know and love. How do they make you laugh? Remember Gilda Radner, or your favorite younger comedians? These folks often have "extreme, but loveable traits" and view the human condition with love and laughter. Read *New Yorker* cartoons. Watch funny things in movies and the monologues on late-night television. Look sideways at mishaps in daily life. You may note that humor is about a brief punch, like the jokes delivered by Bob Hope. It is often direct, but it can be subtle and indirect as well.

Author and commentator Connie Cronley compiled her NPR autobiographical essays into a book: *Sometimes a Wheel Falls Off: Essays from Public Radio*. She once told friends and family "Life is funny. You can be tootling along, carefree and happy, when everything begins to fall apart. A parent dies. A spouse gets sick, and you realize that in life, sometimes when you least expect it, a wheel falls off, and your life changes" (Cronley, 2000, 41). This is the kind of tone readers like on public radio. The subject matter appeals to listeners, who can relate to life crises and gain distance by hearing such treatment of another's problems.

David Sedaris appears often on NPR's "This American Life" and many of his books are compiled from his public radio essays. I find some of them particularly funny, especially his poignant memories of being different in school and having attention focused on him, for example, because he took speech therapy during school hours. One essay on learning French, "Me Talk Pretty One Day," always makes me laugh because I have had difficulties similar to his ludicrous vignettes. The essay ends with Sedaris understanding his teacher—with success! . . . of a sort. As he puts it:

> Understanding doesn't mean that you can suddenly speak the language. Far from it. It's a small step, nothing more, yet its rewards are intoxicating and deceptive. The teacher continued her diatribe and I settled back, bathing in the subtle beauty of each new curse and insult.
> "You exhaust me with your foolishness and reward my efforts with nothing but pain, do you understand me?"
> The world opened up, and it was with great joy that I responded, "I know the thing that you speak exact now. Talk me more, you, plus, please, plus." (Sedaris, 2000, 173)

Here, as usual, Sedaris is able to laugh at himself but explore his very real problems with sensitivity, throwing us a few curve balls along the way. Being able to get the distance to explore your life's difficulties in a lighter vein allows both you and your reader to benefit from your experience, without repeating the suffering so greatly.

▶ *Write Now! Using the Old and New Media*

Try to write a brief, NPR-style essay, but if you are not funny, don't worry. Maybe humor is not something you can do at this point. Try to be generally lighter in your writing, however. Writing is very hard work, so try to lighten up. Otherwise your writing may be so heavy handed that it becomes hard to take. Step back and get some distance. Give yourself permission to write badly; your writing won't always be good, but if you keep going, it will improve and you will have something on the page to revise.

Put your digitized essays and photographs as well as any photographs or home movies you can digitize into an ebook (digitizing video is still expensive, but maybe soon . . .). Programs for creating ebooks are available on the web. One of the best can be found at NightKitchen.com. This program allows you to drag any digitized files onto an icon of a book, easily designing, compiling, and publishing your work. Your ebook can be published on the web, or you can make CDs and sell or distribute them to your friends.

Finally, write a technological literacy autobiography, examining your life's experience with the technologies of communication. How did you achieve your current state of literacy with the media and communication technologies? Conceive of your use of technologies as broadly as possible. ◀

▶ *Read and Discuss Now!*

The following essay is a great exploration of how computers—in this case, computer gaming—can allow users to develop different parts of their personalities or aspects of subjectivities. After you read the essay, discuss with your group how developing characters online can affect your real-world personality. If you were a teacher, would you accept this essay for an autobiography assignment?

Autumn Glave

"Jono The Confused"

Birth in the MUD

I created Jono in my second year at the University of Oklahoma. One evening at about six, I was in the Dale Hall Tower computer lab, killing time while waiting for the Animation Society meeting to start. My friend Anthony wandered in and managed to get a computer next to mine. We talked for a few minutes about this and that, and then we went back to work on our individual computers. After several minutes, I glanced over and saw that he was typing into a weird pop-up window. I asked what he was doing and he said that he was playing a MUD. Then he invited me to join him. I agreed, being very curious about this game. Usually, I stuck to console games rather than computer games because I didn't own a computer myself. It was hard to play any kind of game on the lab computers so I had never really gotten into MUDs.

Anthony showed me how to set up the game and create a character. I pestered him with questions about what the various stats did and he answered impatiently. Finally, I was ready to name my new character. I racked my brains trying to think of a cool name, but everything I could think of was lame. Anthony glared at me impatiently from the seat next to me. I needed a name, any name! My thoughts stumbled over common American names and bizarre fantasy names, but none stuck. *George, that's no good, Fred, no, Darkstar, been done, Joe, no, Theronody . . . wait a minute . . .* "Joe No," I mumbled to myself. "Joeno? Jono!" I smiled with relief as I typed the name into the computer. Anthony just shook his head and muttered, "Took you long enough."

So Jono was born. She was an elven fighter class with only minor magical abilities. The first thing Anthony advised me to do with her was to engage in some practice fights. I quickly learned the simple typed commands and sent Jono out to kill monsters or die trying! I actually had time to fight several low-level monsters before I signed off to go the club meeting.

Over the next couple of days, I grew accustomed to the system of typed commands. Jono fought monsters and explored the town and surrounding country. One of the most interesting things she found to do was to visit the Smurf village and fight the Smurfs. It may sound strange, but the Smurfs were tough opponents. Jono died several times while facing them. As she leveled, she spent most of her skill points in training for physical fighting rather than magic. Similarly, her money was spent on weapons and armor rather than spell books. I started to look at the more complicated parts of the game system.

While exploring the functions, I found that each character could have an epitaph or short description given to it. Immediately, I was captivated by the thought. What epitaph should I give Jono? Who did I want her to be? I thought about her character. She was a fighter not a thinker. I had been ignoring all the major game quests and goals while playing so she tended to wander around randomly and fight monsters. I have a very bad sense of direction so I could never remember what was where. As a result, Jono tended to run into walls and dead ends a lot. Her character was different from the characters I had played in console games. She was more like me, less of a hero and more of an individual. I knew I had to come up with something that would symbolize her individuality, her freedom from the straight and narrow path of herodom, her human flaws. Yet, I didn't want to be too serious. After all it was just a game to me then.

I tried several descriptions, but none of them seemed to work. Most of them screamed "newbie," which I was, but I didn't want other players to look down on me because of my lack of experience. One day I got tired of trying to think of the perfect epitaph so I just typed in "The Confused" after Jono's name and it stuck. I liked the way it sounded and it was obscure enough that no other player was using that epitaph. One day, another character asked Jono why she was confused. By that time, I wasn't really confused, but Jono still was. I think she told the other character something like, "I just am. It makes me happy." Happy confusion, I could appreciate the dynamics of that thought.

After several months, I gradually stopped playing that particular MUD. At first, it was because I went home for Christmas vacation and my parents did not have an Internet connection. After Christmas, it was because I had new games to play for my Playstation. I had come to the conclusion that, while the MUDs were interesting, I preferred graphics to text in my video games. Though I stopped playing the MUD, I still liked the character Jono the Confused. I kept the character in mind while playing other games, but I didn't use that persona again until *Diablo II*.

Diablo II: Once More Onto The Net

In the summer of 2000, I was introduced to what would become my favorite online role-playing game (RPG). I was home for summer vacation and taking a break from work. My younger brothers Caleb and Joshua were playing a variety of games, both on the Internet (my family finally started using real computers) and in real life. One of the games caught my eye. *Diablo II* is a graphics-intensive computer-based RPG that can be played online with other players through the Internet. Blizzard, the company that created *Diablo II*, has its own personal network for game play called Battlenet. The goal of the game is to save the world from Diablo, an immensely powerful demon. The available character types were then a sorceress, paladin, necromancer, amazon, and barbarian. Players can talk to each other, fight each other, from parties or groups, trade items, and interact on several different levels.

I had played *Diablo II* once before that summer, but never online. When creating my character for *Diablo II*, I remembered Jono the Confused and decided to resurrect her character. Unfortunately, Jono was a fighter in the MUD and I wanted her to be a fighter in *Diablo II*, but the only female character types were the sorceress and the amazon. This is one of the limitations of most graphics intensive games—the player has to accept a standard physical image instead of being able to design his or her own character image. The barbarian class, which is the fighter class and able to use swords, is pictured as masculine. After thinking about it, I decided that I would just change my mental image of Jono the Confused and accept the male form. Of course, I could have been a barbarian and still kept my image of Jono as a female, but I didn't want to confuse myself too much. This was actually only the first change *Diablo II* made to my character.

The idea of changing Jono's gender didn't seem like a big thing to me at the time. It was only later that I realized how it changed me. I was used to taking gender for granted— I didn't care enough about other players to consider whether they were male or female behind the mask of their surface characters. However, as I started trying to play like a male character, I found myself trying to measure Jono against other characters, being more aggressive in game play, and being less polite with other players. The Jono I was creating then was after all a barbarian male. I felt like he was much more competitive and selfish than the solitary female elf who wandered through that distant MUD.

The MUD character Jono the Confused was not competitive, not goal focused, and tended to avoid other players. Her nature was easy-going and quiet. Jono the Confused in the *Diablo II* world learned to be completely different. He became intensely competitive because the centrality of other players forced him to try to out do them. The punishments for not being competitive were being looked down on by other players and being vulnerable to attack by player killers (PKs)[1]. *Diablo II* is a very goal driven game so Jono became someone who worked on quests nearly constantly. He became an impatient character who would always want to be on the next part of the quest. He also became someone who is very picky about details. He would spend hours making sure every part of a quest was covered. Barbarians in *Diablo II* have a very aggressive fighting style. The best way to play as a barbarian is to charge into the middle of fights and overwhelm the opponents before they can hit you. Jono became very aggressive and very eager to attack the enemy. This caused problems for me later on in the game because some enemies are too powerful to attack directly. I had to control Jono's instinctive aggression to keep us from dying.

Diablo II online is very focused on player interaction and that fact forced me to consider certain aspects of Jono the Confused's personality. Player interaction is the principal reason for online play so the game was set up to supply

---

[1] A player killer is a player who spends his or her time seeking out and killing other players for fun and profit. Often they prey on characters who are weaker or lower level. They kill the player characters to take their items, boast about their own strength, or to amuse themselves.

better items, stronger enemies, and more experience points to players who played in the same game room as other players. When I realized how important other players, other people, were to the game play, I had to make some decisions about Jono's character. The first choice was whether I would be social or anti-social. I wanted Jono to be sociable because I wanted the extra benefits provided by the game. However, I had problems with certain other characters. During the first month that I played, I was cheated by other players during trades and backstabbed several times. It was enough to make me become less sociable and avoid multi-player game rooms most of the time.

The question with a shared world such as *Diablo II* online is how the players act. A couple of players almost ruined the game for me. I thought that as I continued to play and decided that Jono needed morals. Even if other players decided to be inconsiderate, I could make the game better by being polite. So I made Jono the type of person who would never become a PK, who would help newbies instead of mocking them, and who would not swear at other players or be purposely annoying. However, the lessons I learned about the nature of some other players were also incorporated into Jono. Jono will never trust random strangers with important items, let others steal all the good treasure, or allow people to sneak up behind him.

I still play *Diablo II* as Jono the Confused, though I now have several other Diablo characters as well. My other Diablo characters are patterned on Jono in many ways, including their names: Voire the Vague, Rece the Lost, and Kel the Fallen. However, when I think of Jono today, I think first of Amtgard instead of *Diablo II*.

Jono the Confused in the Real World

In November of 2000, I brought Jono the Confused into the real world. Katie, one of my friends at college, has a boyfriend named Brandon. Both Katie and Brandon are from Texas. Brandon transferred to the University of Oklahoma for the fall semester. I saw him occasionally when I saw Katie, but I didn't spend much time with him at that point. Throughout the semester, Brandon worked on finding people to participate in a sport called Amtgard. He described it as a cross between a medieval fighting/re-enactment group such as the SCA and fantasy live-action role-playing. I still wasn't entirely sure what Amtgard was but I agreed to join because it sounded rather interesting. So on a chilly November day, I got up at 10:30 and headed down to the designated meeting place by the Duck Pond.

A motley group had gathered there. Brandon, of course, and Katie. Anthony was there as were several others that I did not know. The first thing Brandon did, besides learning names, was give a brief run down of the rules of basic combat. He described what blows would wound and which would kill, demonstrated with a padded foam sword, and then set us out to practice. I remember feeling very awkward, yet eager as I gripped the electrical-tape covered hilt of a short-sword and faced off against Anthony for the first round. I won the match because I wasn't hesitant to attack, a trait that may have come from my experiences in Diablo II and other games.

After we practiced until we were thirsty and tired, Brandon started explaining the more complicated parts of the game. Each of us would need a character, a persona, to be during class battles. Amtgard is arranged into classes in a way that is somewhat similar to *Diablo II*. The ordinary classes are wizard, healer, druid, bard, warrior, barbarian, assassin, monk, archer, and scout. Each class has its own special rules, garb (clothing) requirements, and abilities. I looked at the rulebook to try and decide what to be. The magic classes (wizard, healer, druid, and bard) I ruled out because they required the memorization of spells. Archer was out because I didn't have a bow or arrows. Warrior was tempting because there was nothing special to memorize and the warrior gave five lives. Scout was not interesting because usually scouts used bows and were geared towards indirect combat. Assassin and monk both had complicated rules and no throwing daggers were available for use, so I decided against them. It was down to barbarian and warrior. In the end I went with barbarian because I wanted to play as Jono the Confused.

The Jono the Confused of Amtgard is different from the *Diablo II* version in several ways. First, the Amtgard Jono is, once again, a woman. I decided to shift back because it was hard to play a guy in real life. Especially, when I get hit in the chest. Second, Amtgard Jono is much more whimsical and silly than the goal-focused *Diablo II* persona. Jono from Diablo had actually become very responsible when playing with others and would never run off and leave them in the middle of a quest. Jono in Amtgard is someone who might switch sides or wander off if the game becomes annoying. She doesn't feel much responsibility for the other players and has used them as human shields before. Third, the Amtgard Jono is much more evil. I'm more likely to help someone I don't know in an online game than I am to help the friends I play with in real life. The Diablo Jono is not a player killer, while Amtgard Jono will cheerfully kill whoever gets in her way. I think this has to do with the combined nature of the people in our Amtgard shire. We're not exactly heroes—our leader wants to be a necromancer, there are always several assassins around, and we only fight with honor when it's amusing. In *Diablo II*, I don't know any of the other players so there is no way to be evil in a friendly way. Friendly evil is something we have plenty of in Amtgard.

One of the best examples of our nature was what happened at our first coronation feast. The feast took place after a hard day of playing Amtgard. The previous week we had elected new leaders, held several fighting contests, and some craft contests. During the feast we were to celebrate the new leadership as well as watch the awards from the contests being passed out. Rachel and Zeal were hosting the feast at their house and they did a wonderful job. When we arrived, the house was full of delicious smells and a low banquet table was set up in the living room. We all sat down on the floor around the table to wait for the food to be ready. I was in full Jono the Confused mode, talking as if I were a fierce barbarian. A faux wolf-skin was serving as a rug near where I was sitting so I picked it up and wrapped it around me to add to my costume.

We were waiting for the food to be ready and for Steel, aka Mark, to arrive. Steel was our new leader so we couldn't start the feast without him and he was late. Everyone got impatient quickly because none of us had eaten yet that day. I was talking to Khay, aka Anthony, the assassin who was sitting across from me. He happened to mention that one of his special assassin class abilities was to be able to poison food at banquets. I asked him how and he told me that all he had to do was put a red drop on the bottom of the plate or cup he wanted to poison. I dug around in my bag and handed him a red marker. Then we looked around for someone to poison. We were sitting at the end of the table nearest the leader's seat and there was Steel's cup, unprotected and alone on the table.

Khay grabbed the cup and everyone watched him put the red dot on it. Then we went back to waiting for Steel to arrive. Once he came, the feast started. No one said a word as we watched him drink from the cup because if he found out that he had been poisoned, he might have been able to cure himself. Finally, after the five minutes it takes a person to die of poison in under court circumstances, we told him that he was now dead because he had been poisoned. Everyone laughed and made fun of him because he didn't even live long enough to be crowned.

Living with Jono the Confused

Jono has gone through many changes since I first put two random words together to make a name. Changes in gender, changes in attitude, changes in goals. As Jono changed and grew I also felt myself changing. I may not have done anything except play games, but it doesn't matter that they were only games. I put myself into my character and I feel that I have experienced many new things because of this. Being Jono let me look at myself and consider my own good and bad qualities. Then, I could try to improve what I saw. In many ways, what happened to Jono was a reflection of what I was trying to do to myself. Four years ago, I was overly shy and hated to be responsible for anything. I made Jono in Diablo be a bold, courageous, and responsible person because I admired those traits and I was trying to become bolder myself. Now, I am bolder and more willing to take the lead in my own life. By being someone else for a while, I have become more myself than I ever was before I was Jono the Confused. ◀

5

Writing Alternative Futures for the Twenty-First-Century "I"

Ah, the mysterious croak. Here today, gone tomorrow. It's the best reason I can think of to throw open the blinds and risk belief. Right now, this minute, time to move out into the grief and glory.

—Barbara Kingsolver, 1995

Where will you be a year from now? Two or five years? How about a decade down the road? Most if not all of us have no notion. Some people even resist fantasizing or doing too much planning. Yet imagining a possible future can be the first step to bringing your vision or parts of it into existence. A university colleague always fantasized about "graduating" from her job when her son graduated from high school. Recently she was offered a new position in another part of the country, with greater challenge, and she was also accepted to graduate school in computer technology in England. Her active imagining of the future helped these exciting opportunities come to pass.

Imagining a Future

If you never imagine a possibility, even if it is actually *physically* possible for you, it becomes *effectively* impossible. That is because you never open

111

to the possibility and do not act to make space for it in your life. I never considered graduate school until a former professor suggested it—it had never entered my mind! Suddenly, I began to ruminate over what seemed an exciting next step to my career as a journalist. Imagining a future (or alternative futures), then, begins to open things up. Where will you be when you are 25? 30? 40? Brainstorm about even the wildest possibilities. One young woman dreamed of going to a Zen monastery to become a monk. This dream became a reality, and although she died quite young after returning to the United States, her memoirs show that her life was nonetheless fulfilled. What forces make it hard for you to conceive or write about certain future paths?

▶ *Write Now! A Perfect Day*

Designer Milton Glaser asked his School of Visual Arts students to design a perfect day for themselves five years from now. It was to be not simply fantasy but a realistic day that would satisfy them in light of their relationships, work, and physical environment. This is a good activity for writers of autobiography to undertake.

- Imagine such a day for yourself and free-write about it in your journal. Then list your goals as the day reveals them. Identify the information you need to pursue these goals seriously.

- Share your day with your group. You might also write a journal entry about where you hope to be in the future at a "marker" date you set yourself—one, three, five, or ten years away. Who will you be in the future? How would you be different if a different future came to pass? What is your vision of the future? What kind of society would you like (or like your children) to live in?

- What would you be willing to give your life for? What would make your life feel fulfilled even if you were to meet an early death?

Develop one of your journal entries into a longer essay about where you see yourself at some point in the future. When you tackle and complete this assignment, you will have articulated a vision, an imagined future society, and you will have a better idea what you value and aim for in a larger sense. The following essay was written to match an imagined future with civic issues the writer expected to face in the future. Today, she is right where she imagined, working as an occupational therapist.

Bobbi Story (now Miller)

"Issues I Will Be Facing in Ten Years . . . "

I will be getting married in 1½ weeks. As the wedding approaches, I think about what my life will be like. There are many things that come to mind. I wonder how many children I will have and what they will be like. I wonder if I will be out of school and working or staying at home with my children. Although I do not know what my life will be like, I enjoy thinking of how it might be.

Ten years from now I think that I will be living in Kentucky while my husband attends Southern Seminary. I do not think that we will live in a huge house, but I think that it will be large enough for our family. It will have a large enough back yard for the dog to run and play in and for fun family activities. I will be happily married and have a couple of children, maybe a six-year-old and a four-year-old. I will enjoy taking care of my children and will do all that I can to help them with their education and have an enjoyable and memorable childhood. At this time, I will probably still be learning the best way to discipline and encourage good behavior in my children.

One of my children will probably be in grade school. Because I have a child in school, I will face many issues that deal with the school system. I will be concerned with how the school is run, what kind of training teachers are receiving, and how effective the most recent teaching methods are. I will be very interested in the type and quality of education my child is receiving. I will also be more involved in who is elected to the school board, because it will affect my family and me more.

Ten years into the future I will probably either be staying at home caring for my family or working as an occupational therapist. Although I do look forward to completing school and beginning work, I also think of the benefits of not working outside the home. I think that I would enjoy staying at home taking care of my family. Although in ten years I may be at home when the kids are small, when they go to school, I may resume my career as an occupational therapist.

I may be working in a hospital, home health care, or within the public school system. Wherever I work many issues will come my way. I most definitely will be facing the issues that will come up around Medicare. Whether Medicare is increased or not will affect my line of work greatly. Another issue that I will face in my occupation is how well patients are treated while receiving care. This is a strong issue today and will probably continue to be more of concern to others as time passes by.

Around this time, I may also be thinking of having another child. I think that I would like to have three or four children. If this is the case, I will face issues that may come up in the ways hospitals deal with childbirth. I may be facing decisions that have been made in the past or decisions that are made in the near future as to how well newborns and their families are treated while in the hospital or how long the stay in the hospital is. If there are major issues within the hospitals at that time I could very well be affected and become involved in issues of that type.

If I do have children at this time, I will be concerned about issues of safety for children. I will need to know what types of food and toys are beneficial to them. I will be interested in new ways of learning and teaching concerning children. I believe that in ten years there will be many new breakthroughs about individual ways of learning. I will want to keep up to date on these issues so that I can determine if my children would benefit in any way from putting new ideas into practice.

It seems that in ten years, much of my life will be focused on my family, and most of the issues I face will involve them. Although my life will change dramatically over the next ten years, there will still be some things that will remain the same. I will still be concerned with who is elected into the presidency, the senate, and as governor. As I get older, different issues will be of interest to me. The things I encounter as I move on with my life will affect how and what issues concern my family and me. ◀

Autobiographical Manifestos

This section continues this discussion of alternative futures as well as the earlier discussion about multiple roles in our lives and multiple commitments and cares. Who are you now when you are writing? Who might you become? The authorial voice in traditional autobiographies has been described as representing a generic, universal human subject. The author seems to know, solidly, where he has been and where he is going. He assumes that the readers understand him, espouse his values, and willingly join in his life's quest. His subjectivity is whole and unquestioned. The direction of his growth is toward autonomy and independence from others. I use the male pronoun here because autobiographical critics gender this voice as male. (The stereotype for female is, of course, concern for relationships and relatedness over autonomy and isolation.)

Theorists of autobiography such as Sidonie Smith (1983), in *Subjectivity, Identity and the Body*, warn that adopting traditional subject positions can be powerful but may also be dangerous for anyone who does not occupy a secure social position. More and more of us who write have been marginal to traditional literary culture. Smith advises us to watch out, that traditional narrative frames themselves often censor certain bodies, forcing an author to censor herself at times (154). Therefore, adopting traditional voices, styles, and forms can also lead to repeating traditions of oppression, she believes. (Translating "bodies" into "voices" is a curious thing, is it not? Yet it is true that with computer data mining, experts who study writing style can often describe the gender of the text's author.)

Nevertheless, because writing is both social and historical, the voice of the confident Victorian patriarch is beyond most of us today. Times and available "subject positions" for writing change, and this is no longer the nineteenth or even the twentieth century. Perhaps because of the times in which we live, the narrator in many autobiographies today cannot use the same voices or take the same subject positions in autobiographical texts. That is why the author has so often been described as "dead" or at least "fragmented."

Today, we know more about the complexities of our psyches, and our lives and social systems are possibly more complex. Ever since Freud described the subconscious, we have thought of ourselves as less solid and more fragmented. As we saw in the last chapter, our technological capabilities allow us to explore and play with that sense of fragmentation, and many of us do so in our writing. Finally, however, we want to pull ourselves together, explore our world(s) as we confront it (or them) as a single body, inside our skin. This is the only way we can make probable judgments about our experiences and act upon them.

Autobiographical writing can be a helpful process of recognizing the parts of ourselves and pulling ourselves together in print to make those judgments and act.

What forms and styles then are available to capture our more complex, twenty-first-century voices and subjectivities? Smith writes that creating "hybrid" or "resisting" frames can allow a wider variety of subjectivities to be expressed in life narratives. Some of the hybrid, experimental forms have involved mixing chronologies with interviews, biographies of others, articles, photographs, and self-portraits. Genres include testimonials, witnessing of various kinds, prison narratives, and collective autobiographies—that is, autoethnographies or cultural autobiographies. The multimedia forms discussed in the last chapter are a prime source of new genres. Another form Smith advocates is the genre of the autobiographical manifesto. She defines it as follows:

> Dictionary definitions suggest that a manifesto is a proof, a piece of evidence, a public declaration or proclamation, usually issued by or with the sanction of a sovereign prince or state, or by an individual or body of individuals whose proceedings are of public importance, for the purpose of announcing past actions and explaining the reasons or motives for actions announced as forthcoming. (Smith, 1983, 157)

The term *manifesto* means "bring to light," but in the word's root history, there is also the meaning of "strike with the hand." Manifestoes announce the past, explore values, and explain future actions and attitudes. They often explore individuality growing out of identification with a group. This is a good form to use to confront an old identity that was perhaps socially assigned or caused and to speak or perform a new identity, perhaps to speak as one of a group or for a group.

Examples would include a letter from James Baldwin to his nephew in *The Fire Next Time*; the letter is titled "My Dungeon Shook: Letter to My Nephew on the One Hundredth Anniversary of the Emancipation." In this letter, Baldwin explains his attitudes and values on getting along with white people, advising his nephew on how to get along with racist whites without tainting himself with hatred. We see enough of Baldwin's experience with his brother, father, and grandfather in this essay to know how his values were shaped and understand why he advocates the path he does.

In another example, Sidonie Smith (1983, 169) analyzes Gloria Anzaldua's manifesto, *Borderlands/La Frontera: the New Mestiza.* In her essay, Anzaldua constitutes her subjectivity as one who lives along the Texas–Mexico border and who is herself mixed. She has "gone from being the sacrificial goat to becoming the officiating priestess at the crossroads." She explores this notion of her geography at the borderlands as a way to contest the identity given her by society and publicly announce who she is, claiming a more complex subjectivity. Manifestoes such as these are helpful to imitate as part of the process of clarifying our own stances and values.

▶ *Write Now! Reading and Writing Manifestoes*

Read an autobiographical manifesto—Baldwin's or Anzaldua's or Helene Cixous's "The Laugh of the Medusa" or Donna Haraway's "A Manifesto for Cyborgs" or another you find yourself. Discuss with a group how the manifesto fits the definition in this chapter's epigraph. How does it publicly "perform" a new subjectivity? How does it attempt to shape the future? What groups does it identify with? (Note that the readerships often are multiple.)

If you are not yet ready to write a manifesto, work through the next sections exploring ethical values and your body, and see if that helps you clarify and begin to invent a manifesto. If you are ready, however, go ahead and write a manifesto of a few pages.

The following student essay is a manifesto about public issues of body.

Tina Black (Berry)

"Tuesday Afternoon"

I am sitting on my couch at two o'clock on a bright Tuesday afternoon. I think, What a perfect day this has become! I think I will go downtown to have some lunch at my favorite small café. After eating, I will go next door to acquire some new artwork. Nothing big, just a picture of a tiny pink flower in ink. Well, that is after I drive the 3½ hours down I-35 to Dallas, Texas. Within the Oklahoma state borders I cannot enjoy this perfect day the way I really want to.

In 1993 my older brother escorted me to a small shop in downtown Salt Lake City. He introduced me to a tough-looking friend of his who walked me to a back room and unwrapped a few tools from their sterile wrappers. Then he began to etch on my backside a piece of art that I had chosen. A year later, I'm back in that shop, paying for another work of art, and this time it is on my hip. The following year a friend and I learn of a clean and friendly shop in Arkansas. We drive the hour and a half from Stillwater to a small town, eat a nice lunch, shop in a great antique store and then step up to the needle for more beautiful ink. Within three years I have adorned my body with permanent markings of a heart, a sweet cupid, and a dolphin. These are all in places where I have to take down or pull up an article of clothing to show anyone. Even my bathing suit hides all three of them. And I am confident in the aesthetics and ethics of the artists who have tattooed me.

I graduated from high school in 1993 with honors. I currently attend a highly respected university, maintaining a very respectable grade point average as well as working at a full-time job in the health care industry to pay for my own house and car. Despite all the responsibility I put on myself, why am I still not capable of having the responsibility of making a decision about my own body? Within the Oklahoma state lines it remains illegal to give a tattoo. There was talk of legalization beginning the new year making this taboo ritual legal. Despite the rumors, it has yet to be so. I am still unable to go anywhere in the state and obtain a legal tattoo.

The state government has presented its reasons for denying tattoo rights. Government officials have stated that tattooing and other cultural influences such as violence in the media, and offensive music lyrics have led to a deterioration of society. If laws are passed toward legalization there is a possibility of disease transmission through needles. In the past, in other states that have legalized tattooing, there have been outbreaks of hepatitis B, the latest reports being from Dallas, Texas.

In light of the government's obvious concern for my welfare, and yours, I must ask what actions have been made to protect me from everything else that is harmful? What has the government done to stop sex, which transmits numerous diseases and has been proven to lead to corruption, by our own American president? What about dangerous sports such as bungee jumping and parachuting? These can certainly be life threatening. Then we have to stop those who enjoy walking at night. That, too, can be potentially dangerous. It has come time to outlaw everything. If something has any possible consequences that are detrimental to our health, we shouldn't do it, ever.

Is that what this has all boiled down to? No, at least I hope not. That is why we have laws and government regulations. I consider the piercings that I have, most of which are visible. Piercing is legal in Oklahoma, uses needles, and is much more invasive than tattooing. Yet there are laws that piercing shops must abide by to remain open, and they do remain open. We have laws that forbid sex with minors. An individual can be charged with manslaughter if he or she knowingly transmits the deadly HIV virus to another person. Condoms are highly recommended for those who are sexually active and are even handed out in some high schools, though forbidden at the public school I attended. There are regulations of the outdoor adventure organizations, and they must take responsibility for their actions, having clients sign waivers, and taking safety precautions in potentially dangerous situations. Other states that have legalized tattooing have made laws such that anyone getting a tattoo must be 18 years of age and free from any alcohol and/or drug influences. There are health codes that tattoo parlors must meet and maintain. In some states the laws are so strict that few shops are able to exist and must keep higher pricing than other states, but they are nonetheless allowed to exist.

I would not dare allow anyone to place a needle on me outside of completely sterile conditions. A tattooist's studio should be as clean as, or cleaner than, any doctor's office and just as conscious of contamination. Guidelines can and should be set before Oklahoma passes laws allowing tattoos. But these laws should be passed. It is our right as citizens and as individuals to have this option. Within Oklahoma there are still people getting tattoos every day. They may be in their best friend's bedroom with a homemade tattoo gun or in the basement of "some guy" they heard about from a friend of a friend of a friend. No basis of regulation exists for these tattoo "artists" to follow except for their own personal ethics and morals, which not everyone has.

Most people are very accepting of tattoos in this day and age. They are as common place as jewelry, hats, and briefcases. Those who are offended most often refer to the big biker with arms sleeved in tattoos. The same big guy with all the tattoos might be offended by a stuffy businessman in suit and tie. I recently viewed a study done over the Internet. A student at a university held an on-line poll to see what people thought about tattooing. Upon tabulating the results she was surprised to find out how many people were accepting of what she found offensive. As I was further checking out the Internet I found the home page for the high school I graduated from. I found a section on the page with the opinions of students on tattoos. Not only was the overall opinion accepting, but even the teachers who responded didn't think it was a big deal as long as individuals investigated what they wanted to have printed on their bodies for the rest of their lives as well as where they got the work done.

The way I see it, the general population does not seem to rally against tattooing, those who want tattoo shops have great support, and it is highly possible to make laws and regulations to control the tattooing industry for health reasons. So why does the state government still refuse to allow tattoo shops to open? I am quick to say that tattoos are not for everyone. It is a matter of choice and personal taste. It is time for the government to wake up and deal with these issues. Those who wish for legalization should start to direct inquiries to the state government. All I want is to have the option of going down to my favorite shop on a Tuesday afternoon or any other day and getting that cute little flower tattooed on my toe. And I prefer to do it without having to cross state lines.

Discuss how this student has combined personal life narrative and argument into a manifesto-like essay? Is it effective? Could it be made more effective? How? ◀

Values Toward the Future

Autobiographical writing can help clarify our values and commitments by helping us define and pinpoint what we really care about. Carol Bly (1998, 39), in *The Passionate, Accurate Story*, theorizes that humans are "programmed for ethical consciousness." She advocates an exploratory activity to help us identify our values, what we feel about a subject. Here are some activities she shares to get you started reflecting on your values:

- First, write down "two goals or values which make life good or bearable or would if they were in operation."

- Second, write down two goals or values that cause injustice and suffering or lessening of joy.

- Third, put down two missing goals or behaviors, those that as a child, you thought that grown-up life would have. (A close friend volunteered that as a child, she always thought adults would share a "life of the mind." Today as a philosopher, she is disillusioned to find few around her to talk with about serious matters.)

- Fourth, list "two injustices which you see about you" and that you feel you should keep an eye on, "even on your wedding day."

Share these with a group and talk about them. Did any of your group members' values surprise you?

The subtitle of Bly's book is "Making Your Heart's Truth into Literature." Identifying values is one way of putting your finger on your heart's truth and desires. It is also a good start for thinking about the kind of future you'd like to live in. Both of these can be worked into literature by journaling about values, then writing a manifesto based on an aspect of your values.

Embodiment

One of the formative aspects of yourself that is overlooked by many people has to do with how you are embodied. This includes your skin color and ethnic features as well as your distinctive differences—your body as it is. Your body is something that changes throughout your life and that you perhaps imagined in thinking about your future life. Has your body materialized in your writing to date?

Smith and Watson (2001, 175) pose questions for readers to ask about the body in autobiographical narratives: "Precisely when and where does the body become visible in the narrative? Which part, or functions, of feelings of the body? How does it become visible? What does that visibility mean? How are the narrator's body and its visibility tied to the community from which the narrator comes?" We can usefully ask ourselves or those in our writer's group the same questions about the body in our own texts.

Many memoirs about disability feature the body. Two I have especially enjoyed are Nancy Mairs's *Waist-High in the World* and Lucy Grealy's *Autobiography of a Face*. It is easier to see how writers whose bodies are visibly different from mainstream bodies could focus on how embodiment affected them. Yet all of us are in part created by our different bodies, which change as they mature, age, and improve or decline at various points in our lives. Creative nonficton writer Phillip Lopate (2002, 105) tries to get at some of the meanings of his body in his essay "Portrait of My Body." It begins:

> I am a man who tilts. When I am sitting, my head slants to the right; when walking, the upper part of my body reaches forward to catch a sneak preview of the street. My lousy posture, a tendency to slump or put myself into lazy, contorted misalignments, undoubtedly contributes to lower back pain. For a while I correct my bad habits, do morning exercises, sit straight, breathe deeply, but always an inner demon that insists on approaching the world askew resists perpendicularity.

The essay takes up most of his body parts, ending: "Whatever narcissism, fetishism, and proud sense of masculinity I possess about my body must begin and end with my fingers" (112). (It is not clear by this point that he is really talking about his fingers!)

▶ *Write Now! Our Bodies Now and in the Future*

- Write a portrait of your own body after Lopate's model or revise another paper to add embodiment where you feel it would contribute. It may help to take one part of your body, such as your teeth, and do a 10-minute journal free-write, adding more parts as you go along.

- Envision your future body and fantasize about its maturing or changing. (Do not assume it will necessarily decline as you age—some people grow stronger or learn to take care of their bodies as they age.)

- Create for yourself a virtual body in cyberspace. How does it change your view of your body to imagine re-creating it in a computer world without gravity or physical space? Look at the virtual bodies in Vesna's Bodies INCorporated project, which explores how we shift our perceptions of our bodies when we incorporate ourselves in a networked environment. Or create your own. See http://vv.arts.ucla.edu/projects/current_events_frameset.htm. ◄

Autobiographical Writing: Growth and Development

Autobiographical writing can support personal and individual as well as social and civic development in writers. We have seen that authors of personal autobiographical writing need not make a forced choice between becoming a richer individual or a more compassionate contributing member of society, because that is a false choice. The two go hand in hand, and it is not possible to have one without the other. Becoming aware of the sometimes narrow and egocentric focus of our mind gives us the opportunity to broaden our view and become more socially conscious. We begin to understand how our stories and meanings are intertwined with other people's stories and meanings. The process of constructing a narrative can help us shape, name, and evaluate our experience. The process of reflecting on our lives can help us grow in personal and social awareness.

Becoming mindful of how we have been shaped by living in a particular body, time, and place also shows us how things could be otherwise. In not taking the world and its experience so much as solid, brute fact but asking how things came to be the way they are, we can also ask how they could be better. We can ask how improvements in our world would allow us to be better people. We notice how we participate in constructing our public world through our private values and choices.

Recently, for example, some California students decided to buy sports clothing that cost about a dollar more than their usual brands because they learned that the company making it was committed to paying workers a living wage. Through their reflections on the world, the students decided it was in their own best interest for companies to pay more because it was good social insurance—more people would be able to support their families and wouldn't have to be supported by the state. They were thinking in a future-oriented mode.

In her research, my colleague Dr. Irene Karpiak is finding that autobiographical writing helps adult writers grow through a process of self-exploration and meaning making, transforming their view of themselves and the world. Watching our own processes of growth can also give us distance and space for us to lighten up, show compassion for others, and let the anger and rage that inevitably comes up through daily interaction fall apart more quickly. It gives us a solid basis for maturing—and acting and judging accordingly. Personal writing in a mindful way allows us to get some distance on ourselves and enjoy the space to unfold.

Traveling, Travel Writing, and Growth

Travel is one of the most growth-producing experiences we can have. Many college students have traveled a little, and some older or returning students may have traveled extensively. New college students often "leave home" to go to college, a life-changing experience that parallels travels or moving. Nothing provides more insight into who we are culturally and individually than travel, and few things are more insight-provoking than the dislocations, stresses, and joys of learning to adapt to a new place. Because of these factors, travel can be spiritually stirring and worthy of autobiographical writing.

▶ Write Now! Writing on the Move

- List places you have been. Did you keep a travel journal or write about any of your travels? Use photos or meditate on your trips to recall details.

- List places you want to go. Read some travel literature or search the web to learn about one of the places you would like to go.

- Keep a travel journal of the land and cultures of the places you visit over the next year, even if only on weekend trips to nearby towns and attractions. Make it a project in autoethnography. You might also focus on a particular theme, such as food and practices of agriculture, marketing, cooking, and presentation. ◄

Toward a "Next" Stage of Autobiographical Writing

Now you have much serious writing and thinking going on. An important thing to do while you are writing is to take the time to read memoirs and autobiographies by others. Keep a list of favorites on a shelf in your bookshelf for "books that inspire." You can start with some of the works in the Bibliography or start browsing in local bookstores. Most have a section for memoir and autobiography, but these books may be scattered throughout the store. Keep writing for yourself, for your family and friends, and for the pleasure of working with memory and crafting your life into art. Write to share, write to publish, write for the record, write for therapy. Write for insight—to create significance and read meaning into life events. Write to create alternative futures.

Here are some autobiographical writing suggestions:

- Complete and polish several of the shorter inventional exercises in this book.
- Finish all five "chapters" of your autobiography.
- Present short pieces on a website, with visuals.
- Publish humorous vignettes, radio essays, articles, or an autobiography.
- Keep a journal for life and living.

More Writing/Journal Prompts from Students

My undergraduate students regularly turn in ideas for journal or free-writing prompts on index cards. You might benefit from a few of their ideas:

- Write about a turning point in your life
- When you first realized your parents weren't perfect
- The first time your heart was broken by a friend or romantic interest
- A dream
- A favorite or least favorite pet
- A big storm
- What you have learned from a hobby or volunteer activity
- Music that moves you
- How your grandparents met, fell in love
- Your spiritual life as a child
- Getting into trouble
- Love and madness
- Embarrassing moments
- A difficult choice you made
- Your major
- Family traditions
- Sibling tortures
- Best and worst gifts
- Beginnings and endings, transformation, such as breakups or divorce
- Fears and crises
- Foods—cooking, eating, favorite memories of meals
- Favorite fictional character
- Regrets
- Struggles over being different
- Special friends
- Places you have lived, including neighborhoods, and how they formed you
- Family sayings

Reading Others' Autobiographical Writing

Here are some guidelines created by one of my undergraduate classes on how authors and readers should work with writing in its formative stages. These guidelines might help when you are working in groups, but your reading and editing groups may want to make their own ground rules!

1. Make constructive criticism, being sure you criticize the text you are reading, not the writer or the writer's life choices.

2. As a writer, be open to criticism. Writers must learn that criticism of their work is not personal!

3. As a writer, if you are unsure about sharing a particular piece, don't share it! Bring the group only pieces you feel comfortable sharing, and don't mind the constructive criticism they might receive.

4. For each bit of criticism offered, make a suggestion on how to improve and enhance the piece. Don't forget to praise the good parts!

Publishing Your Writing

This book has been about the inventing and crafting of life narratives, but at some point you may want to think about publishing your memoir or portions of it. In Chapter 4, we saw that web publication of various sorts is a real and creative possibility. Another new genre, the ebook, is another way to publish and distribute autobiographical material. Traditional outlets should not be overlooked, however. Some newspapers publish short personal columns, and editors may agree to publish notices that you have published your autobiography or interview you about it. You may find a publisher or self-publish a book of memoir. Magazines are a more likely forum for personal writing, however; several publish chapter-length or shorter autobiographical narratives. The following resources may help you find places to publish your work:

- *A Writer's Guide to Copyright.* Caroline Herron, ed. Published by Poets and Writers Press.
- *International Directory of Little Magazines and Small Presses.* Names and addresses of smaller or regional presses that publish memoirs.

- *Writer's Market.* An annual publication listing conventions for querying publishers as well as names and addresses for major publishers.
- *Writer's Guide to Magazine Markets: Non-fiction.* Provides even more details about specialized material published by magazines.
- *The Literary Marketplace.* A directory of U.S. book publishers.

Know that even if you never publish widely or with a substantial publisher, writing and sharing your life writing—whether through traditional print manuscripts or new media, such as a personal blog—can be a satisfying and growth-producing activity and can allow you to continually unfold as a writer and a human being.

Bibliography

Acker, Kathy. "Dead Doll Humility." *Postmodern Culture* 1.1 (Baltimore: Johns Hopkins UP, 1990).

Ameringer, Oscar, 1870–1943. *If You Don't Weaken: The Autobiography of Oscar Ameringer, with a Foreword by Carl Sandburg.* New York: H. Holt, 1940.

Anzaldua, Gloria. "Borderlands/La Frontera: The New Mestiza." In *The Norton Anthology of Theory and Criticism.* Vincent B. Leitch, Gen. ed. New York: Norton, 2001. 2211–23.

Baldwin, James. *The Fire Next Time.* 1962. New York: Dell, 1969.

Bakhtin, Mikhail M. *The Dialogic Imagination.* trans. Michael Holquist and Caryl Emerson. Austin: U of Texas P, 1981.

Barrington, Judith. *Writing the Memoir: From Truth to Art.* Portland: Eighth Mountain P, 1997.

Bly, Carol. *The Passionate, Accurate Story: Making Your Heart's Truth into Literature.* Minneapolis: Milkweed P, 1998.

Carroll, Lewis. *Through the Looking Glass and What Alice Found There.* 1872. London: Penguin, 1994. Also at Project Gutenburg, http://www.cs.indiana.edu/metastuff/looking/ch8.html.gz, Milennium Fulcrum Ed, 1991.

Cixous, Helene. "The Laugh of the Medusa." In *The Norton Anthology of Theory and Criticism.* Vincent B. Leitch, Gen. Ed. New York: Norton, 2001. 2039–56.

Couser, G. Thomas. *Vulnerable Subjects: Ethics and Life Writing.* Ithaca: Cornell UP, 2004.

Cronley, Connie. *Sometimes a Wheel Falls Off.* Tulsa: HAWK Publishing, 2000.

Dillard, Annie, and Cort Conley. *Modern American Memoirs.* New York: HarperCollins, 1995.

Dillard, Annie. *Holy the Firm: A Journey into the Beauty and Violence of Life.* New York: Bantam, 1977.

Dubrow, Gail Lee, with Donna Graves. *Sento at Sixth and Main: Preserving Landmarks of Japanese American Heritage.* Seattle: Seattle Arts Commission, 2002.

Ede, Lisa S. and Andrea Lunsford. *Singular Texts, Plural Authors: Perspectives on Collaborative Writing.* Carbondale: Southern Illinois UP, 1992.

Fisher, Ada Lois Sipuel. *A Matter of Black and White: The Autobiography of Ada Lois Sipuel Fisher.* With Danney Goble. Foreword by Robert Henry. Norman: U of Oklahoma P, 1996.

Folkenflik, Robert, ed. *The Culture of Autobiography: Constructions of Self-Representation*. Stanford: Stanford UP, 1993.

Foucault, Michel. *History of Sexuality, Vol. 1*. Robert Hurley, trans. New York: Vintage, 1990.

Franzen, Jonathan. "Personal History: My Father's Brain." Sept. 10, 2001, *New Yorker*, Sept. 10, 2001, 81–91.

Freedman, Diane P., and Olivia Frey, eds. *Autobiographical Writing Across the Disciplines*. Durham: Duke UP, 2003

Gilmore, Leigh. *The Limits of Autobiography: Trauma and Testimony*. Ithaca: Cornell UP, 2001.

Goldberg, Natalie. *Long Quiet Highway*. New York: Bantam Books, 1993.

Haake, Katharine. *What Our Speech Disrupts: Feminism and Creative Writing Studies*. Urbana, IL: National Council of Teachers of English, 2000.

Hart, Moss. *Act One: An Autobiography*. New York: Vintage, 1976.

Hogan, Linda. *The Woman Who Watches Over the World: A Native Memoir*. New York: Norton, 2001.

Houston, Jeanne Wakatsuki, and James D. Houston. *Farewell to Manzanar: A True Story of Japanese American Experience During and After the World War II Internment*. 1973. New York: Dell, 1995.

Howe, Nicholas. *Across an Inland Sea: Writing in Place from Buffalo to Berlin*. Princeton: Princeton UP, 2003.

Jefferson, Margo. "On Writers and Writing: The Stuff of Legend." *New York Times Book Review*. Sec. 7, Col. 1, p. 27, March 14, 2004.

Jelinek, Estelle C. *The Tradition of Women's Autobiography: From Antiquity to the Present*. Boston: Twayne, 1986.

Karpiak, Irene. "Writing Our Life: Adult Learning and Teaching Through Autobiography." *Canadian Journal of University Continuing Education* 26.1 (2001): 31–50.

Kelton, Nancy Davidoff. *Writing from Personal Experience*. Cincinnati: Writer's Digest Books, 1997.

Kim, Elaine H. "Defining Asian American Realities through Literature." *Cultural Critique* 6 (1987): 87–111.

Kingsolver, Barbara. *High Tide in Tucson: Essays from Now or Never*. New York: HarperCollins, 1995.

Kress, Gunther. *Literacy in the New Media Age*. New York: Routledge, 2003.

Krupat, Arnold, and Brian Swann. *Here First: Autobiographical Essays by Native American Writers*. New York: Modern Library, 2000.

Labov, William. *Language in the Inner City: Studies in the Black English Vernacular*. Philadelphia: U of Pennsylvania P, 1972.

Lamott, Anne. *Bird by Bird: Some Instructions on Writing and Life*. New York: Anchor, 1995.

Lejeune, Philippe. *On Autobiography*. Foreword by Paul John Eakin. Trans. Katherine Leary. Minneapolis: U of Minneapolis P, 1982.

Lopate, Phillip. "Portrait of My Body." In *The Fourth Genre: Contemporary Writers of/on Creative Nonfiction*. Robert L. Root Jr. and Michael Steinberg, eds. New York: Longman, 2002.

McCarthy, Mary. *Memories of a Catholic Girlhood*. 1946. San Diego: Harcourt Harvest, 1985.

Moffett, James. "Writing, Inner Speech, and Meditation." *College English* 44.3 (1982): 231–46.

Nafisi, Azar. *Reading Lolita in Tehran: A Memoir in Books*. New York: Random House, 2004.

Nunberg, Geoffrey. *The Way We Talk Now*. New York: Houghton Mifflin, 2001.

Olney, James, ed. *Memory and Narrative: The Weave of Life-Writing*. Chicago: U of Chicago P, 1998.

———. *Studies in Autobiography*. New York: Oxford, 1988.

———. *Autobiography: Essays Theoretical and Critical*. Princeton: Princeton UP, 1980.

Ostrom, Hans, Wendy Bishop, and Katharine Haake. *Metro: Journeys in Writing Creatively*. New York: Pearson Longman, 2000.

Postman, Neil. "Questioning Media." In *The Wired Tower: Perspectives of the Impact of the Internet on Higher Education*. Matthew Serbin Pittinsky, ed. Upper Saddle River, NJ: Prentice Hall, 2003. 181–200.

Rohman, D. Gordon, and Albert O. Wlecke. *Pre-Writing: The Construction and Application of Models for Concept Formation in Writing*. East Lansing: Michigan State U Cooperative Research Project No. 2174, 1964, U.S. Office of Education.

Rousseau, Jean-Jacques. *Confessions*. 1782. Trans. Angela Scholar, ed, with intro and notes by Patrick Coleman. New York: Oxford UP, 2000.

St. John, Warren. "Dating a Blogger, Reading All About It." *New York Times*, Sunday Styles Section 9, p. 1, 11. Sunday, May 18, 2003

Sanchez, Raul. "Composition's Ideology Apparatus: A Critique." *Journal of Advanced Composition* 21.4 (2001): 741–59.

Schlegel, Friedrich. *Athenaeum*. 1798. In *Dialogue on Poetry and Literary Aphorisms*. Trans. Ernst Behler and Roman Struc. University Park: Penn State UP, 1968, p. 143.

Scholes, Robert, Nancy R. Comley, and Gregory Ulmer, eds. *Text Book: An Introduction to Literary Language*. New York: St. Martin's Press, 1995.

Schultz, Heidi. *The Elements of Electronic Communication*. Boston: Allyn & Bacon, 2000.

Sedaris, David. *Me Talk Pretty One Day*. Boston: Little, Brown, 2000.

Simpson, Caroline Chung. *An Absent Presence: Japanese Americans in Postwar American Culture, 1945–1960*. Durham: Duke U P, 2001.

Smith, Sidonie. *Moving Lives: 20th-Century Women's Travel Writing.* Minneapolis: U of Minnesota P, 2001.

———. *A Poetics of Women's Autobiography: Marginality and the Fictions of Self-Representation.* Bloomington: Indiana UP, 1987.

———. *Subjectivity, Identity, and the Body: Women's Autobiographical Practices in the Twentieth Century.* Bloomington: Indiana UP, 1983.

Smith, Sidonie and Julia Watson. *Reading Autobiography: A Guide for Interpreting Life Narratives.* Minneapolis: U of Minnesota P, 2001.

Stillman, Peter. *Families Writing.* Cincinnati: Writer's Digest Books, 1989.

Tan, Amy. "Memory: 'My Mother.'" *New Yorker*, Dec. 24 & 31, 2001, p. 83.

———. *The Bonesetter's Daughter.* New York: Ballentine, 2001.

Unsigned Note/Review. Connie Chronley. *Sometimes a Wheel Falls Off: Essays from Public Radio. Tulsa University Alumni Magazine.* Winter, 2000, 41.

Verene, Donald Phillip. *The New Art of Autobiography: An Essay on the Life of Giambattista Vico Written by Himself.* Oxford: Clarendon, 1991.

Weathers, Winston. *An Alternate Style: Options in Composition.* Portsmouth, NH: Boynton/Cook, 1980.

Finding Helpful Websites

Search with a search engine using keywords "autobiography studies," "life writing," and other terms such as "autobiographical studies," "oral history," "memoir," "diary," and so forth. There are also bibliographies, online journals, and other materials, such as "American Life Histories: Manuscripts from the Federal Writer's Project." One helpful site is at www.hawaii.edu/biograph. An autobiography listserv is also available at Hawaii. Remember, the web is always changing, so check it out for yourself.

Credits

Student Readings

Chapter 2
Bonner Jack Slayton, "Is This Who I Am?"
Kelsey Marie Martyn-Farewell, "What's in a Name?"
Monica Guadelupe Gomez, "Acrostic"

Chapter 3
Tara Stine, "World Events and My Life"
Kevin Fischer, Milestone Journal-Writing: "Timeline Event"

Chapter 4
Autumn Glave, "Juno the Confused"

Chapter 5
Bobby Story (Miller), "Issues I Will Be Facing in Ten Years"
Tina Black (Berry), "Tuesday Afternoon"

Index